Deep Alberta

FOSSIL FACTS AND DINOSAUR DIGS

ROYAL TYRRELL
MUSEUM

THE UNIVERSITY OF
ALBERTA PRESS

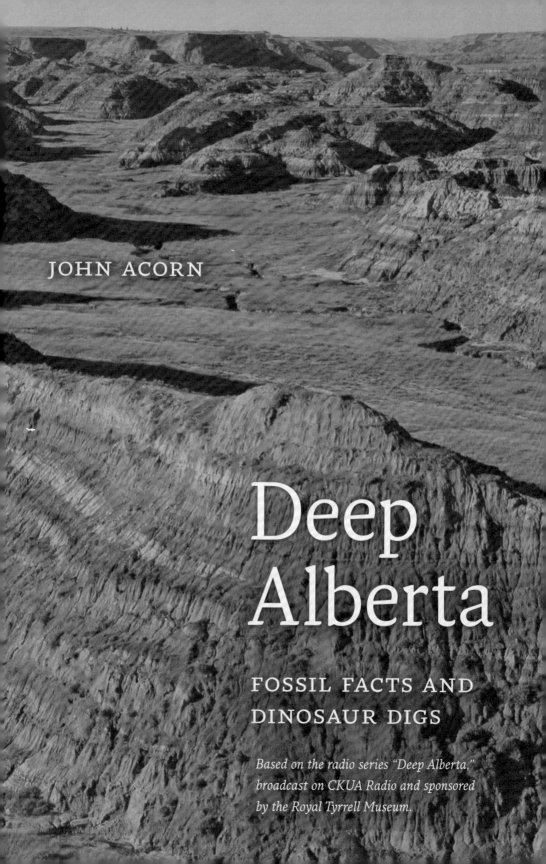

JOHN ACORN

Deep Alberta

FOSSIL FACTS AND DINOSAUR DIGS

*Based on the radio series "Deep Alberta,"
broadcast on CKUA Radio and sponsored
by the Royal Tyrrell Museum.*

Published by

The University of Alberta Press
Ring House 2
Edmonton, Alberta, Canada   T6G 2E1

and

The Royal Tyrrell Museum
PO Box 7500
Drumheller, Alberta, Canada   T0J 0Y0

Copyright © Royal Tyrrell Museum of Palaeontology/Alberta Community Development 2007
Printed and bound in Canada by Houghton Boston Printers, Saskatoon, Saskatchewan.
First edition, second printing, 2009
All rights reserved

LIBRARY AND ARCHIVES CANADA CATALOGUING IN PUBLICATION

Acorn, John, 1958-
    Deep Alberta : fossil facts and dinosaur digs / John Acorn. — 1st ed.

Co-published by: Royal Tyrrell Museum.
Includes bibliographical references and index.
ISBN-13: 978-0-88864-481-7

    1. Paleontology—Alberta. 2. Dinosaurs—Alberta. 3. Fossils—Alberta. I. Tyrrell Museum of Palaeontology
II. Title.

QE748.A4A36 2007   560.97123   C2006-906916-6

The University of Alberta Press and The Royal Tyrrell Museum gratefully acknowledge the support received
for its publishing program from The Canada Council for the Arts. The University of Alberta Press also gratefully acknowledges the financial support of the Government of Canada through the Book Publishing Industry
Development Program (BPIDP) and from the Alberta Foundation for the Arts for our publishing activities.

Contents

Acknowledgements

For palaeontological assistance I would like to thank Dennis Braman, Don Brinkman, Jim Burns, Michael Caldwell, Pat Cavell, Philip Currie, Dave Eberth, Greg Erickson, Richard Fox, Jim Gardner, Murray Gingras, Gavin Hanke, Kirk Johnson, Paul Johnston, Takuya Konishi, Eva Koppelhus, Jim McCabe, Mark Mitchell, Raoul Mutter, Bruce Naylor, Andy Neuman, Dale Russell, Michael Ryan, Craig Scott, Ruth Stockey, Darren Tanke, Mark Wilson, and Gord Youzwyshyn. Others who helped in other ways include Karen Linauskas, Sharon Cross, Judy Dunlop, Brian Dunsmore, Bev Hodson, Sonia Kochansky, Laura Jackson, Wendy Johnson, Amber Nicholson, Elaine Secord and Dena Stockburger. I would also like to thank Linda Cameron, Michael Luski, Alan Brownoff, Cathie Crooks, Yoko Sekiya and Peter Midgley, all of the University of Alberta Press, for their continued support of my work.

Introduction

SO WHAT, EXACTLY, IS "DEEP ALBERTA?" Well, the way I see it, Deep Alberta is the prehistoric heritage that places our province in context in what geologists and palaeontologists call deep time. In 2005, when the Royal Tyrrell Museum and CKUA Radio approached me with the idea of a radio series about Alberta palaeontology, I was enthusiastic about the project and set about choosing 80 topics, each of which became the subject matter for a short radio broadcast. As the scripts accumulated, it became apparent that we had the makings of an interesting book as well.

In choosing subject matter for this project, I was able to draw from Alberta's rich dinosaurian legacy, as well as tremendous riches from the geological time period following that of the Cretaceous dinosaurs, the Palaeocene. Fortunately, our province also preserves a record of life during the much more recent "Ice Age," as well as much older fossils and sediments that are exposed on the surface in such places as the Rocky Mountains and the far northeast corner of Alberta, on the Canadian Shield. Certainly, much has been left out, but it is my hope that by reading the accounts that follow, you will find yourself developing a solid general understanding of the fossil heritage of Alberta, and the pieces will begin to fall together and create a meaningful whole. After all, that is exactly what palaeontology does best.

Some of the topics that follow are famous, obvious aspects of Alberta palaeontology—things like the dinosaur nests at Devil's Coulee, or the massive extinct predator *Albertosaurus*. Others will surprise most readers, since they have not been the subjects of much popular attention up to now. In choosing these subjects, I have tried to reflect not only the composition of the fossil record, but also the interests and discoveries of palaeontological researchers in Alberta, not just at the Royal Tyrrell Museum, but from around the province wherever such discoveries are made. I was also keen to pay homage to the early fossil hunters and geologists who first uncovered Alberta's ancient legacies and whose names are forever associated with many of our extinct plants and animals.

And finally, it is my hope that those of you without a formal background in palaeontology will find here some interesting insights into the inner workings of this fascinating discipline. Without an understanding of the nature of scientific names, the reconstruction of evolutionary relationships and the geological history of the Earth, the stories of fossils lose much of their relevance to a broader appreciation of life on Earth. But with some relatively simple fundamentals, they become part and parcel of a wondrous story, "billions of years in the making," as we boasted on CKUA.

Geology of Alberta

This map shows the age of the rocks either at the surface or just beneath the clay, sand and gravel deposits that were laid down during the Ice Age.

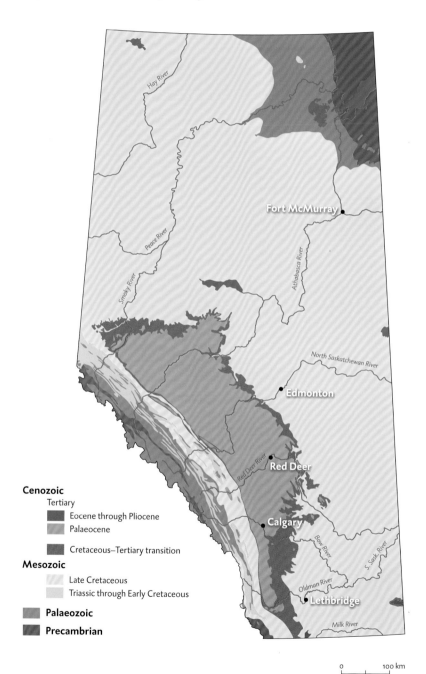

Cenozoic
Tertiary
  Eocene through Pliocene
  Palaeocene

  Cretaceous–Tertiary transition
Mesozoic
  Late Cretaceous
  Triassic through Early Cretaceous

Palaeozoic

Precambrian

0   100 km

Albanerpetontids, as We Say...

LET ME BEGIN BY TELLING YOU about a subject that, at least so far, only palaeontologists care about—the Albanerpetontidae. Why? Well, I figure that learning something this obscure should help you realize that the world of palaeontology contains vastly more detail, and more wonderful evidence, than any one person could ever comprehend. So what is an albanerpetontid? In short, it's a type of extinct amphibian. But not just any amphibian, a lissamphibian—like all of the living amphibians, and quite unlike the early amphibians, that were so important before the Age of Dinosaurs. Today, we have frogs (including toads), salamanders and caecilians making up the Lissamphibia (and I suppose I should explain what a caecilian is—it's a legless amphibian from the tropics, not an Italian person from the island of Sicily). So, along with the three groups of living amphibians in the Lissamphibia, there were also the extinct albanerpetontids, which you could also call allocaudatans if you so chose. There are at least a dozen types of these creatures known, dating back the Jurassic Period, and if they were alive today, it is likely that we would all mistake them for salamanders.

Now, if you could get inside the head of an Alberta palaeontologist, more than likely they would not be fantasizing about time machines and *T. rex*. Instead, you might find yourself contemplating the pattern of skull bones that make albanerpetontids different from true salamanders. This fundamental difference inspired Dr. Bruce Naylor, the director of the Royal Tyrrell Museum, along with his mentor, Dr. Richard Fox of the University of Alberta, to formally name the Albanerpetontidae as a separate group in 1982. More recently, Dr. Jim Gardner, the Tyrrell's collection manager, working with Dr. Márton Venczel of Romania, has identified the last surviving albanerpetontids from Pliocene-aged rocks in Hungary—they were only 5 million years old. In other words, at coffee time at the Royal Tyrrell Museum you can imagine what they talk about—not just the spectacular and the newsworthy, but also the infinite details that make up the fossil record of life on Earth, and connect us with deep time, and Deep Alberta.

*The front of the face and
a few jaw fragments of
albanerpetontids—
not much to go on, but
important nonetheless.*

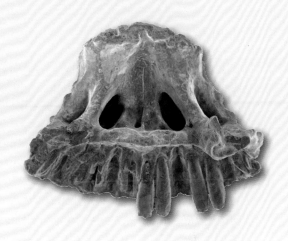

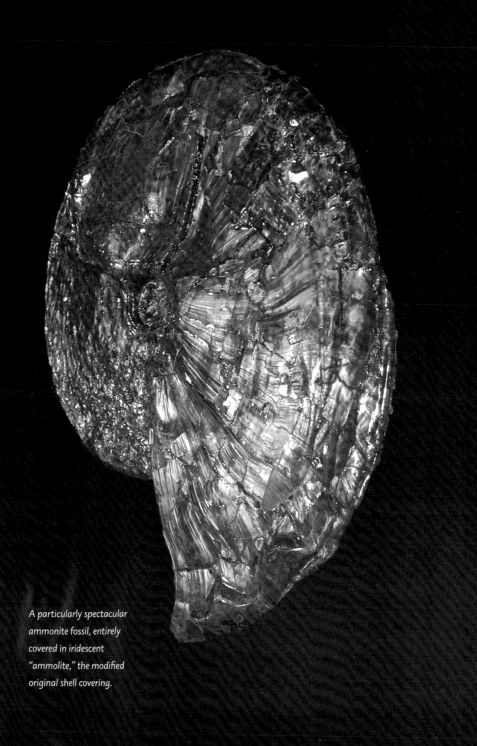

A particularly spectacular
ammonite fossil, entirely
covered in iridescent
"ammolite," the modified
original shell covering.

Ammonites and Ammolites

WHENEVER YOU SEE A RECONSTRUCTION of life in the sea during dino-saur times, there are ammonites in the picture. You probably know what they looked like even if you don't recall the name. Ammonites had tenta-cles like an octopus or a squid and they lived in shells. Octopus and squid are members of the group called cephalopods and they do have living rela-tives with coiled shells, the nautilus. But ammonites were not quite the same as nautilus. For one thing, not all ammonites had coiled shells. Some of the ammonites had straight shells and some had shells that were sort of coiled, but the coils were "open" and not joined to one another.

In Alberta, there are plenty of ammonite fossils from the Cretaceous Period, the last part of the Age of Reptiles. You can recognize the straight-shelled ammonites because the shells often break apart into their component chambers. The actual animal lived in its first and largest chamber, and the rear chambers were closed off and filled with gas for buoyancy. Where the chambers join, the outer wall of the joint is a complex, curly suture line that is very beautiful even in the fossils.

Coiled ammonites are also found here in Alberta. They are easy to recognize once you have seen a few, and in the most impressive of these specimens the fossil shells display an iridescent covering of altered shell material that was laid down when the shell was growing. This irides-cence is now called "ammolite" and is the basis of a jewellery industry here in Alberta, in which ammonite shells are made into such things as rings and brooches. The ammolite excavators frequently donate speci-mens that might be important to science and alert palaeontologists about other sorts of fossils that turn up in their quarries. For some palaeon-tologists, seeing a fossil as a piece of jewellery is a terrible shock, but to others it shows that the fascination for these remnants of the past is not limited to those with formal or academic motivations. That a fossil can be both profoundly old and profoundly beautiful is, to me, profound. Ammonites, by the way, very nearly went extinct during the Permian extinction just before the Age of Reptiles, although they seem to have been declining before that, and to have recovered quite well afterwards. The final extinction of the ammonites occurred along-side the last of the dinosaurs, and like the dinosaurs, they seem to have been declining before it happened, at least here in North America.

Albertosaurus, Alberta's Dinosaur

THE FOSSIL BEDS OF THE ALBERTA BADLANDS are the last resting place of some very famous creatures—*Tyrannosaurus rex*, *Triceratops*, and a host of other dinosaurs from the last period—the Cretaceous—of the dramatic Age of Reptiles. But the dinosaur Albertans should know best is the huge predator that bears our province's name—*Albertosaurus sarcophagus*. *Albertosaurus* was basically a half-sized version of *Tyrannosaurus rex*, built for speed and agility, measuring some seven metres in length and weighing in at a modest tonne and a half. The *sarcophagus* part of *Albertosaurus'* name means—literally—that it ate dead animals and this, at times, was probably the case. But this fearsome predator was also surely able to make kills of its own. Its ten-centimetre teeth were recurved and lined with meat-cutting serrations, and they were fearsome weapons. Balanced on a massive two-legged frame, *Albertosaurus* had a familiar look seen in dozens of large carnivorous dinosaurs over a 150,000,000-year time span—a look that is echoed in giant killer birds that roamed South America millions of years after the last dinosaurs went extinct. The name *Albertosaurus* is now one hundred years old and was first put forth by the legendary American palaeontologist, Henry Fairfield Osborn, in 1905, the year Alberta became a province, and the year Osborn named *Tyrannosaurus rex*. Take note, however, that the correct name is Albert-O-saurus, not Albert-A-saurus, an apparent misspelling that owes its origins to the quirks of Latin grammar.

There are in fact two species of *Albertosaurus*. *Albertosaurus sarcophagus* lived quite near the end of the Age of Dinosaurs, alongside *Tyrannosaurus rex*. *Albertosaurus libratus*, on the other hand, lived ten or more million years earlier. This early *Albertosaurus* was originally named *Gorgosaurus*, until it was shown to be extremely similar to its later relative. Some palaeontologists have resurrected the name *Gorgosaurus*, and you will hear it from time to time even in a modern context. Although *Albertosaurus* appeared on Earth before its huge cousin *Tyrannosaurus rex*, it was apparently not the ancestor of the so-called "King of the Tyrant Lizards." That distinction may well go to another large predator, the big-boned, broad-headed *Daspletosaurus*. All of these dinosaurs are part of the same family, the tyrannosaurids, named for their most famous member. So the herbivores of the Late Cretaceous had a host of giant predators to deal with back

A complete (and completely impressive) skeleton of Albertosaurus libratus *on display at the Royal Tyrrell Museum.*

then, just as we have four big cats that prey on herbivores in North America today. It's a fair guess that other dinosaurs were not awed or impressed by *Albertosaurus* and its kin, but today they are symbols of primitive power and grace, living on through their fossils and inspiring people the world over to marvel at the fossil treasures of the past.

A biting midge
(Ceratopogonidae) from
Alberta amber—not all
dinosaur-age blood-suckers
were mosquitoes.

Amber, Fossilized Tree Sap

AMBER IS FOSSILIZED TREE SAP and it is often the most beautiful of fossils. I love it myself, and I often look for amber jewellery to buy for my wife. But the most interesting bits of amber are those with insects inside. After all, it's not unusual for bugs of various sorts to become mired in tree sap. In Alberta, amber is a fairly common fossil, especially in rocks that also contain coal, but most of our amber is so crumbly that it turns to powder the instant you try to remove it from the rock. One site, however, produces very high quality amber from the Late Cretaceous, about 75 million years ago. This location, in the Lethbridge area, has yielded hundreds of fossil creatures, including beetles, bugs, flies and spiders. Polishing the amber and examining each specimen for bugs is a very time-consuming task and it takes a long time before you actually know if you have found anything. In the movie *Jurassic Park* irresponsible money-hungry scientists extract dinosaur DNA from the stomach of a fossil mosquito trapped in amber. They then use the DNA to clone real dino-saurs, in a process that sounds not only plausible but also downright easy. But could it be done? Well, at the time the film was made there were no mosquitoes known from the Age of Dinosaurs, but that all changed when my long-time friend Ted Pike discovered a mosquito in Alberta amber and made headlines around the world. Ted wasn't trying to clone dino-saurs, but the connection was obvious and thus the find became famous overnight. To look at it, you would think that every last detail of Ted's mosquito was perfectly preserved, down to the finest hairs on the segments of its tiny antennae. But, in fact, amber insects are mostly hollow shells, preserving the outside appearance of the insect, but not much of the inner organs at all. Some researchers have apparently extracted insect DNA from amber fossils, but even these claims have come under scrutiny lately by those who believe that the data is far too easy to misinterpret, and far too easy to become contaminated by other more recent sources of DNA. So sleep well tonight, and have no fear that mad scientists are cloning *Tyrannosaurus* on uncharted tropical islands, even though an Alberta discovery brought the storyline of *Jurassic Park* one step closer to reality.

Amia, The Bowfin

AMIA—WHAT SORT OF FOSSIL CREATURE MIGHT THAT BE? It sounds like it has a friendly, "amiable" name, doesn't it? Well, the name *Amia* is actually a Greek word referring to certain sorts of Greek fishes, but today biologists use the name for one particular sort of North American fish, the bowfin, *Amia calva*. The living bowfin is found over much of the eastern United States and in southern Ontario and Quebec. It is a long, narrow fish with a powerful bite and an elongated dorsal fin along the top of its body. Anglers enjoy catching bowfin, but they don't generally eat them—apparently bowfin taste pretty bad, unless they are smoked. But they fight hard and in many ways bowfin are tremendous survivors. They live in quiet shallow backwaters and they gulp air when the water is low on oxygen. This fish's equivalent to a lung is a swim bladder that takes oxygen directly from the air (the swim bladder is also a sort of internal body-balloon that allows fishes to regulate how heavy they are in the water). Some fishermen think bowfin are a nuisance, since they appear to compete with sport fish such as bass, but others see them as a harmless natural part of the ecosystem. Although we have no bowfin in Alberta today, fossils of fishes from the bowfin family are common, especially from the Palaeocene Epoch, just after the Age of Dinosaurs. We often find their characteristic large scales and their small conical teeth, and in some areas even partial skeletons are common. In fact, it appears that while there is only one species of bowfin on Earth today, the ancient world was populated with a great diversity of bowfin species. They were found around the world, and thus the living bowfin is now a living fossil. Next time you visit the east and your fishing buddies curse the bowfin on their line, remind them that bowfin are yet another interesting part of our deep palaeontological heritage.

The bow-shaped smile of a long dead bowfin fish whose fossil remains were found along the Blindman River in central Alberta.

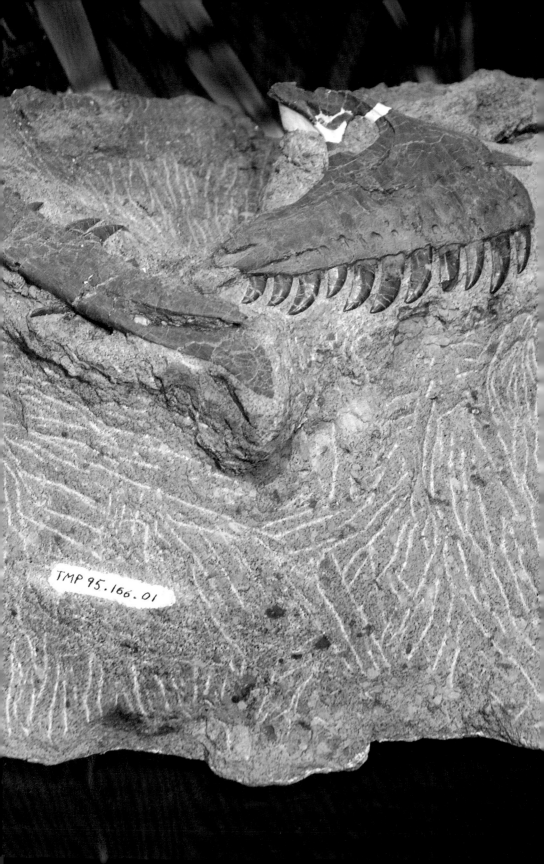

TMP 95.166.01

Atrociraptor, The New Raptor

THE WORD "RAPTOR" is Latin and it can mean either grabber or robber. Biologists who study living animals usually think of raptors as birds of prey, such as hawks, eagles and owls. Palaeontologists, on the other hand, use the word raptor to refer to a variety of carnivorous dinosaurs with sharp teeth and long-clawed grasping hands. The newest addition to the raptor clan is *Atrociraptor marshalli*. So far, this dinosaur is known only from a single partial skull, discovered only 5 km from the Royal Tyrrell Museum. It was a small dinosaur, with a skull only about 17cm long, but it is clearly different from its near relatives, especially with respect to the depth of its snout—it was a relatively short-nosed sort of raptor. The two men who named this dinosaur are Phil Currie, a professor at the University of Alberta and a research associate of the Royal Tyrrell Museum, and David Varricchio of the Museum of the Rockies in Montana. They chose the name *Atrociraptor* because it means "savage robber," and the name *marshalli* to honour Wayne Marshall of East Coulee, Alberta—the man who found the specimen. *Atrociraptor* was a member of the dinosaur family Dromaeosauridae, and to be honest *any* new fossils from this group of dinosaurs are bound to generate interest from both the public and the scientific community. Not only were "raptors" the stars of such movies as *Jurassic Park*, they were also quite closely related to the dinosaur ancestors of birds. In fact, some of these dinosaurs had feathers and it is reasonable to suggest that *Atrociraptor* did too. Of course, *Atrociraptor* lived during the Cretaceous Period, about 100 million years after the first birds appeared during the Jurassic Period. However, their similarity to birds and the fact that they were members of a diverse group of bird-like dinosaurs living *alongside* birds make the *Atrociraptor* and other raptors the favourite dinosaurs of the popular and scientific media alike.

The one and only specimen of Atrociraptor—a partial skull discovered just down the valley from the Royal Tyrrell Museum.

Basilemys, A Very Large Turtle

LET ME TELL YOU A LITTLE STORY about *Basilemys*. Of course, I don't expect you to recognize the name right away, since *Basilemys* was a great big turtle that lived alongside the dinosaurs during the Cretaceous Period in Alberta's deep history. *Basilemys* was the largest turtle ever to live in Alberta. The shell of an old, wise *Basilemys* could be a metre long and up to seven centimetres thick. That puts *Basilemys* in the same general size range as many sea turtles and giant tortoises, but *Basilemys* was not a member of either of these two groups. Instead, it was either a fresh water turtle or, more likely, a land turtle with a shell that was low and sleek, not domed like that of a land tortoise. Where does *Basilemys* fit in the overall scheme of turtledom? Well, it has taken a long time to sort this out. It appears that it was part of a group of turtles, related to the soft-shelled turtles, that bears the name Nanshiungchelyidae (a reference to the fact that these turtles are

The short, flat snout and stubby legs of Basilemys look a lot like those of living land tortoises, but its shell was low and sleek, like that of a water turtle.

also known as fossils from China, not to mention other parts of Asia, and western North America). It was related to soft-shells, but not at all like them in its habits, since soft-shelled turtles are highly aquatic and fantastic swimmers. What did *Basilemys* eat? Based on the shape of its beak, probably plants, like a modern land tortoise. In the year 2000, Dr. Don Brinkman of the Royal Tyrrell Museum excavated not one but two skeletons of *Basilemys* in Dinosaur Provincial Park in southern Alberta. Finding two together was a mystery in itself, and adding to the puzzle was the fact that one turtle was crushed, as if a two-tonne duck-billed dinosaur had stepped on it by accident. It's a great story if it proves to be true, but it's more interesting from the turtle point of view than from the dinosaur point of view, if you ask me. Not only that, these turtles are partly buried in volcanic ash, leading us to wonder if this might be another explanation for their death.

A steppe bison moseying its way across the Bering Land Bridge on its way to colonize North America some 500,000 years ago.

Bison, As Opposed to Buffalo

IN MODERN-DAY NORTH AMERICA, the largest land mammal is the bison. A big bull can weigh a full tonne, about the same as a medium-sized dinosaur. Now, most people know that "bison" are not the same as "buffalo," since real buffalo live in Asia and Africa, and most people know that huge herds (of 50 million or more bison) once roamed the North American prairies from Alaska to Mexico, only to be very nearly wiped out by European colonists in the 1800s. Now, we have only small herds of both plains bison and wood bison in such places as Elk Island and Wood Buffalo National Parks in Alberta. That's the *history* of bison in Alberta, but the *pre*-history is also fascinating. The first bison originated in Asia, and crossed over the Bering Land Bridge during the Ice Age, some half a million years ago or more. These were the steppe bison, with larger bodies, longer hair, and much larger horns than their modern relatives. One sort of steppe bison had horns that could span more than two metres from tip to tip! Over the course of the Ice Age, the steppe bison gave rise to slightly smaller, more gregarious, smaller-horned bison. The extinct Western Bison, *Bison occidentalis,* is a common fossil bison in Alberta, and around 4000–5000 years ago it was replaced (or perhaps evolved into) the modern sort of plains bison. And in Europe, there is a separate sort of bison living today, the wisent, that appears to have evolved separately from steppe bison ancestors. No one seems quite sure about the details of the evolutionary history of bison in North America, but we do know that in Alberta we have fossils representing each stage in the process. And there are some people who would like to see the bison return to the Alberta prairie and take back their former place in the grassland environment. It's hard to say if the thundering herds could ever return, but it would certainly make a drive down the Trans-Canada Highway more eventful, don't you think?

The Blindman River

YEARS AGO, I was driving down Highway 2 with a couple of palaeontology students, on the way to Drumheller and the Royal Tyrrell Museum. As we passed the turnoff for Blackfalds, one of the students asked if we had time to visit the famous fossil localities in the area. "Well," I replied, "it depends on how high the Blindman is today." The other student then became noticeably nervous. "Who is the blind man?" she asked, "...and what happens when he's high?" Well, of course, I was referring to the Blindman River. It's more of a creek really, and as this small river winds through the aspen parklands of central Alberta it exposes rocks of Palaeocene age, from the time in Earth history about 10 million years after the great end-Cretaceous Extinction that killed the last of the dinosaurs. The fossils from these sites are generally small and unspectacular, but they are nonetheless important to science. The Blindman River fossil sites were originally discovered by Dennis Wighton, an amateur fossil hunter, and as a result the sites are named such things as DW1, DW2, DW3, and so on. It was, however, Dr. Richard Fox and his students at the University of Alberta who studied these fossils. *Saxonella crepaturae*, a tiny primate without close living relatives, was a remarkable find in 1984, since *Saxonella* primates were previously known only from France. This supported the theory that Europe and North America were connected during the Palaeocene Epoch. In 1991, Dr. Fox discovered a second species of *Saxonella*, and named it *Saxonella naylori*, after Bruce Naylor, who is now the director of the Royal Tyrrell Museum. Around that time, I was working for the Canadian-Chinese Dinosaur Project and I recall escorting a Chinese palaeontologist on a trip to the Royal Tyrrell Museum. On the way from Edmonton to Drumheller, we engaged in a somewhat stiff conversation about farming and the Alberta landscape. On the way back, since we had some extra time, I asked if he would like to see the "DW2 site." Suddenly, he was smiling and enthusiastic, and I could hardly keep up with him as he charged through knee-deep snow, broke through the ice of the river in his business shoes, and touched the river banks with trembling hands, saying over and over again, "*Saxonella...Saxonella!*" When he left for the airport the next day, he said his formal goodbyes to my colleagues and then walked over and embraced me, thanking me again for showing him this famous, famous place.

A lovely bend in the Blindman River valley and the famous but fragmentary jaws and teeth of Saxonella naylori.

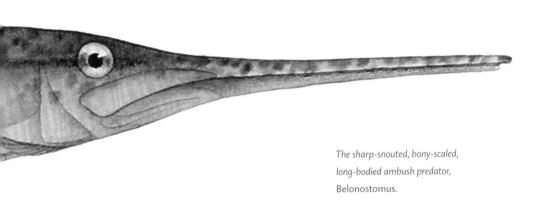

The sharp-snouted, bony-scaled,
long-bodied ambush predator,
Belonostomus.

Belonostomus, A Pointy-headed Fish

DURING THE TIME OF THE DINOSAURS IN ALBERTA, there were weird and wondrous fishes swimming in the Bearpaw Sea, and the rivers that flowed into this northern extension of the Gulf of Mexico. Some, like gar, bowfin, and sturgeon, have living relatives today. But not *Belonostomus*. *Belonostomus* was a smallish, slender fish, and if you were able to travel back in time and catch one, it would probably make a decent meal for only one person, assuming that they tasted good. Their scales were thick and hardened, unlike most modern fish scales. The most obvious thing about *Belonostomus*, however, was its sharp, pointed snout or "rostrum," formed from the tip of the upper jaws. This was clearly a predatory fish, with its fins set far back on the body, like those of a pike. Fish with this body shape generally feed by darting out from ambush and grasping other fish by surprise. The sharp rostrum of *Belonostomus* is a bit of a mystery, but it is possible that it used the rostrum to spear its prey. In fact, it's hard to imagine *Belonostomus* attacking other fish without spearing them, even if by accident! *Belonostomus* had a mouth filled with sharp teeth, and in fact, its jaws are common fossils in the Alberta badlands, easily recognized by the characteristic groove in which the teeth were set. The family to which *Belonostomus* belongs was distributed worldwide and fossils of *Belonostomus* itself have been found as far away as Chile. Its close relatives have been found as fossils in Antarctica. Palaeontologists believed that these fishes all went extinct with the last dinosaurs at the end of the Cretaceous Period, but in 1987 the characteristic jaw fragments were found in North Dakota, suggesting that *Belonostomus* had survived at least another 8 million years. To most people, *Belonostomus* was "just a fish," but it is evidence like this that makes the story of the Late Cretaceous extinction more complicated, and more interesting, than it would be if all we cared about were dinosaurs.

Barnum Brown, Fossil Hunter

BARNUM BROWN WAS A DINOSAUR HUNTER, and one of the most famous figures in the history of dinosaur studies in Alberta. He was an American, born in Kansas in 1873, on February 12—Abraham Lincoln's birthday. Named after the famous circus promoter, P.T. Barnum, Barnum Brown had something of the showman in himself as well. Brown worked for the American Museum of Natural History in New York, and it was his job to lead fossil-hunting expeditions into what was then the "wild west" of Wyoming, Montana, and Alberta. He was the first major-league fossil hunter to explore the Alberta badlands, and worked along the Red Deer River from 1909 to 1915. Travelling on a flat-bottomed barge with a canvas tent perched on top of it, Brown and his team collected a fantastic series of dinosaur specimens that were eventually shipped back to New York. It was Brown's success that inspired the Canadian government to work harder at keeping "our" dinosaurs "here," although at first "here" meant Ottawa, not Alberta. Today, we have casts of many of Barnum Brown's most famous dinosaur fossils at the Royal Tyrrell Museum, but we have also been able to follow up on some of Brown's unfinished work. For example, Brown found the now-famous *Albertosaurus* bonebed in Dry Island Buffalo Jump Provincial Park, where the bones of many of these large meat-eating dino-saurs came to rest in one place. Since the bones were jumbled, Brown passed most of them by, looking for display specimens instead. Barnum Brown was the discoverer of *Tyrannosaurus rex* and the person who named such famous dinosaurs as *Ankylosaurus*, *Corythosaurus*, and *Leptoceratops.* When he died in 1963, at 90 years of age, his legacy was assured.

Barnum Brown (left) and Henry Fairfield Osborn (right), looking both stylish and comfortably cool while excavating a huge dinosaur leg bone in 1902.

The banks of Burbank, where
layers of grey Palaeocene-aged
rock occasionally produce
small but remarkable
fossil treasures.

Burbank, Alberta

FOR THOSE WHO ENJOY FISHING AND CAMPING in the Red Deer area, Burbank—or Burbank Junction as it is sometimes called—is a familiar recreational hotspot. This is the place where the Blindman River meets the Red Deer River and it is nothing at all like the badlands farther downstream. Burbank is, however, a well-known location for fossils. High on the banks of the Red Deer River at Burbank lie the fossils of clams, snails, fishes, mammal teeth, and especially insects—"water bugs" so to speak. These fossils, like all fossils from the Red Deer area, date from the Palaeocene Epoch, after the Age of Dinosaurs, and are around 55–60 million years old. As you walk along the river's edge at Burbank, you might notice that some of the rocks that have tumbled down from above have numerous clam and snail fossils in them. This is what drew the attention of a Red Deer rock hound, the late Betty Speirs, and it was largely through her efforts that these fossils came to the attention of scientists. I remember stopping at the Speirs' house 25 years ago when I was a university student on a palaeontology field trip. There, Betty Speirs had laid out her latest finds on a great long table, and our professors examined each one while we waited. The important specimens made their way back to the University of Alberta, and it was clear that Professors Fox and Wilson were very thankful to Betty Speirs. She seemed more interested in helping these scientists than in keeping the fossils for herself, and for that I admired her. According to the Red Deer River Naturalists, however, in recent years the Dickson Dam has caused changes in the flow patterns of the Red Deer River, and so ice rafts no longer cut deeply into the riverbanks during spring breakup. This has resulted in many of the best fossil sites being covered by plant growth, and to be honest, if there's one thing palaeontologists hate, it's a lush green blanket of plants on top of perfectly good fossil-bearing rocks.

Calgary, and the Things That Lay Beneath It

NEITHER OF ALBERTA'S TWO LARGEST CITIES is known for its fossil riches, but while Edmonton lies on top of bedrock from the end of the Age of Dinosaurs, Calgary lies on top of rock from the next stage in Earth history, the Palaeocene Epoch (from 55–65 million years ago). Over the years, fossils of clams, snails, the teeth and jaws of small mammals, and the tracks of a large mammal have been found in Calgary at sites near the airport, as well as near the city centre. As a matter of fact, one fossil locality, where a new species of multituberculate mammal was discovered in the 1920s, is now underneath an apartment building. Recently, another interesting fossil from Calgary turned up. A man in Carstairs purchased some landscaping boulders from a construction site in Calgary, and when he placed one of the boulders on his front lawn, it split in two. There, inside, was the shell of a fossil turtle. Now fossil turtles from the Palaeocene Epoch are actually quite rare, so when he reported the find to the Royal Tyrrell Museum, their turtle specialist, Dr. Don Brinkman, was quite excited. Don recognized immediately that the turtle shell was not from either a snapping turtle or a soft-shelled turtle, both of which were well known from that time period in southern Alberta. After removing of some of the overlying rock, and numerous fish scales, he realized he was looking at a macrobaenid. So what's a macrobaenid, you ask? It's a sort of fresh-water "sea turtle"—in other words it looks like a sea turtle, and might even be closely related to sea turtles, but doesn't live in the sea. At about three-quarters of a metre in length, this is an impressive animal, at least for a turtle. There are no macrobaenids on Earth today and they remain some-what enigmatic even among turtle specialists. So there you go, a macrobaenid from Calgary—yet another fossil treasure from the deep history of our province. And yes, the Royal Tyrrell Museum did get a new rock for the man in Carstairs.

The macrobaenid "freshwater sea turtle" from Calgary, surrounded by fossil fish scales, each of which has been outlined in black ink.

Camelops, *the extinct North American camel, eyes the tusk of a deceased wooly mammoth, and wonders what it all might mean.*

Extinct Camels

I LIKE SAND DUNES, but in Alberta most of our best dunes are off-limits, on the Suffield Military Base northwest of Medicine Hat. In Manitoba, however, Spruce Woods Provincial Park is filled with huge moving dunes. Nearby, in the town of Glenboro, they have erected a giant cement camel—after all, dunes and camels go together, right? But were there ever camels in this part of the world? The answer, excitingly enough, is "yes," and they lived not too terribly long ago, right up to the end or near the end of the Ice Age some 10,000 years ago. This should be your first clue that camels and deserts don't necessarily go together. In fact, it appears that camels originated in North America and became widespread in the grasslands and open forests here long before they spread to Asia and Africa. One common fossil camel is *Camelops*, the extinct western camel. *Camelops* ranged all the way from Alaska to Mexico, and they grew to be larger than the living camels today. Native people knew them well, but camels were never domesticated in North America as far as we know. The last North American camels went extinct at the end of the Ice Age, along with many other large animals. Camels are related to such things as vicuñas, llamas, alpacas and guanacos, all of which share that odd, three-lipped look with a split upper lip. These latter animals are all South American now, and indeed the diversity of camel-like creatures in South America is still greater than in the Old World, where only two species of camels survive today. In the mid 1800s, by the way, a good number of camels were imported to the United States and Canada, since they showed great promise as beasts of burden—stronger than a horse, and able to withstand everything from frigid winters to blistering heat. The idea didn't catch on, for various reasons (mostly having to do with the fact that no one, horses included, really liked the camels), but the camels found themselves right at home here, as well they should.

The Canadian Shield

So how deep does Deep Alberta really go, anyway? The oldest rocks in the province are in the Canadian Shield, way up in the northeast corner, near Wood Buffalo National Park and Fort Smith. Now, the Canadian Shield is nothing new to eastern Canadians, since it covers huge portions of Ontario and Quebec, as well as northern Saskatchewan, Manitoba, the Northwest Territories and Nunavut—about half of Canada. But here in Alberta, it is a rare geological phenomenon that few people get to see. The Canadian Shield is also called the Precambrian Shield, since it dates from the Precambrian Era that extends back from about half a billion years ago all the way to more than four billion years ago and the beginnings of life on Earth. In Alberta, the rocks of the shield are about two billion years old, which is very, very old. Palaeontologists and geologists get accustomed to dealing in vast ages and immense antiquities, and sometimes they take them for granted. I find that I easily underestimate the real age of fossils and rocks, perhaps because "two thousand" sounds a lot like "two million" or "two billion." But it would take a thousand two millions to make two billion, and a million two thousands to make two billion. In human terms, two hundred years is a long time, and it would take ten million two hundreds to make two billion. In other words, it's worth the mental effort to remind ourselves just how old "two billion years" really is. Unfortunately, the rocks of the Canadian Shield in Alberta have not produced fossils, or if they have, I have never heard the news. That far back in time, however, the only possible fossils would be those of single-celled prokaryotes, or bacteria-style life forms. Of course, just because bacteria are primitive doesn't mean they are inadequate in any way. The history of life has not meant the replacement of so-called primitive life forms with more advanced designs—it has meant the appearance of new and wonderful creatures alongside the tried and true, with plenty of extinction all along this so-called spectrum. In other words, even the terrible drama that Darwin called the "struggle for existence" is in some ways quite forgiving.

One of the oldest rocks in Alberta, and a scene from the Canadian Shield in Ontario, showing the typical patchwork of rocks, trees, and sparkling clear lakes.

The skull of Centrosaurus (foreground), twisted by the forces of fossilization, but with plenty of twisted horns to start with.

Centrosaurus, A Herding Horned Dinosaur

CENTROSAURUS WAS A HORNED DINOSAUR, much like *Triceratops*. But while *Triceratops* was just plain huge, *Centrosaurus* was a medium-sized dinosaur, probably weighing only a tonne and a half at most. *Centrosaurus* also lived before *Triceratops*, during the late, but not latest, part of the Cretaceous Period. For that reason, its fossil remains are common in Dinosaur Provincial Park, where the rocks date from about 75 million years ago. To picture *Centrosaurus*, think of the rhino-like body of *Triceratops*, with the long, but not too long, tail. Imagine the big bony frill that extends back over the neck from the skull, giving the horned dinosaurs huge heads for their body size. But whereas *Triceratops* had two long horns over the eyes, and a short horn on the nose, *Centrosaurus* had the opposite—short horns over the eyes and a long horn on the nose. Some *Centrosaurus* skulls also show curved horns at the back of the neck frill. In the 1970s, Alberta's top dinosaur scientist, Phil Currie, began a long-term study of a fascinating assemblage of *Centrosaurus* specimens in Dinosaur Provincial Park, the so-called *Centrosaurus* bonebed. There, numerous jumbled skeletons of this dinosaur were preserved together. The question was, what happened? Were they travelling as a herd when they died? Did they try to cross a river in flood, and then perish the way caribou sometimes do today during their heroic migrations? Or is this something we can never truly know for sure? About the only thing we do know is that the last thing that happened to these *Centrosaurus* bones was that a flooding river deposited them together some time after the animals had died and started to decompose. The rest of the story will officially remain a palaeontological mystery, although the story of the migrating herd and the flooding river has already become a bit of a dinosaur cliché here in Alberta.

Champsosaurus, A Kind of Non-Crocodile

WHEN IS A CROCODILE NOT A CROCODILE? When it's a *Champsosaurus*, of course, and *Champsosaurus* was a common fossil reptile in Alberta. Fossils of this two-metre long creature have been found in rocks from the Late Cretaceous (alongside dinosaurs) and also from the early part of the Age of Mammals. In other words, like real crocodiles, *Champsosaurus* was not affected by the mass extinction 65 million years ago. Fossil hunters in Alberta are familiar with the shape of *Champsosaurus* vertebrae, especially since they have a characteristic hourglass-shaped mark on their top surface. *Champsosaurs* were probably fish-eaters, and they had a long snout lined with sharp teeth. This makes them most like the living gharials of Asia. But while the gharials are related to crocodiles, *Champsosaurus* was a member of a distantly related group of reptiles. When two distantly related animals come to resemble one another we call it convergence, or convergent evolution. Presumably, to be a successful medium-sized, fish-eating reptile with four legged ancestors, you need to develop a long snout, slender pointed teeth, and a crocodile-like body with a long swimming tail. In other words, you need to look like either a gharial or a *Champsosaurus*. There are differences, however, and anyone can see that the eyes of *Champsosaurus* are much farther forward on the head than those of crocodilians. Many aspects of *Champsosaurus* were therefore presumably unlike what we see in living gharials, crocodiles, and alligators—the true crocodilians. For example, in Montana researcher Yoshihiro Katsura has examined two supposedly separate species of *Champsosaurus* and suggested that they are in fact male and female of the same species. Not only that, the female is better suited to walking on land, since she had to lay eggs on land, while the male could remain in the water hunting fish. Young *Champsosaurus* were also highly aquatic, and it appears that the features that made adult females better at terrestrial locomotion developed later in life—a minor but interesting example of an aquatic animal "returning to land" so to speak, not only in terms of its evolution, but also in terms of its development from birth to adulthood.

Champsosaurus—clearly a swimming predator, but just as clearly not a crocodilian.

Small horns and a long but frail-looking neck frill make Chasmosaurus *a relatively easy dinosaur to recognize.*

Chasmosaurus, A Short-Horned Dinosaur

AMONG THE HORNED DINOSAURS, *Chasmosaurus* never quite achieved
the celebrity status of its relatives the huge *Triceratops*, the spike-frilled
Styracosaurus, or the stump-nosed *Pachyrhinosaurus*. But *Chasmosaurus*
is an important Alberta fossil and a famous dinosaur in its own right.
Looking at a *Chasmosaurus* skeleton (and there are two in the Royal Tyrrell
Museum galleries) the first thing most people notice is that the horns
on the nose and over the eyes of this horned dinosaur were rather small.
This gives it a rather sleek, long-headed look and the very long neck frill
extending from the back of the skull enhances this impression further. Not
only that—the frill is also quite flimsy-looking with huge holes in it, and
is supported only by a slender framework of bone. Some palaeontologists
have looked at this and suggested that it wasn't much good for protection, but could possibly have served as a display. Thus, you sometimes see
paintings of *Chasmosaurus* with their noses tilted down, their frills tilted up
and gaudy colourful patterns on the frills to intimidate or woo their fellow
Chasmosaurus. Perhaps they displayed to one another in order to sort out
which *Chasmosaurus* belonged to which species. It appears that there were
not one but three species of *Chasmosaurus* in Alberta about 75 million
years ago, and all three have left a total of 21 skulls in the rocks of the
Dinosaur Park formation: *Chasmosaurus belli* was named for Walter Bell of
the Geological Survey of Canada; *Chasmosaurus russelli* was named for the
Canadian palaeontologist Loris Russell; and *Chasmosaurus irvinensis* was
named for the town of Irvine near Medicine Hat. It may seem unlikely that
there were three species of similar dinosaurs living in the same place at the
same time, but we do have two almost identical deer, the White-tailed and
the Mule Deer, living alongside each other in the same places today.

North American Cheetahs

YOU MAY HAVE HEARD THE SHOCKING NEWS that there were lions in
Alberta when the first people appeared, but did you also know about the
cheetahs? Yes, there were also cheetahs, right up until a mere 12,500 years
ago. Cheetahs are unusual cats, and they have to be in order to run up to
110 kilometres per hour to set the all-time record for the speed of a land
animal. They have less retractable, shorter claws than other cats and they
achieve their great running speed by flexing their backbone in ways that
other cats simply cannot manage. The early North American cheetahs were
somewhat larger than the living species and may have been faster as well.
On the other hand, the last surviving North American cheetah, *Acinonyx
trumani*, was a bit smaller, but not by much. As far as I know, no fossils of
the extinct cheetah have actually been recovered from Alberta, but they are
known from much of the United States and, after all, they are rare. Perhaps
they never made it this far north. But they did leave their mark on our province, and you can see the evidence even today. Consider the American
pronghorn, sometimes called the prong-horned antelope. It is the *second*
fastest land animal on Earth and can run 100 kph for short bursts. In other
words, it is vastly faster than any of its predators. The American biologist
John Byers has suggested (and most of us believe him) that the pronghorn
evolved in response to the North American cheetah. When the cheetah
went extinct, the pronghorn was left with this wonderful adaptation. Some
people have even suggested that we should "bring back" cheetahs to North
America but I disagree. The pronghorns won, fair and square, and I think
we should leave them alone. Not only that, it may be that the living cheetah
is only distantly related to the fossil cheetahs of North America. Until
recently, palaeontologists believed that cheetahs originated here in North
America, and made their way to Africa after the fact. But a recent paper
in the journal *Current Biology* suggests that the two groups of cheetahs
evolved from separate ancestors, and that based on their mitochondrial
DNA, the North American cheetahs were actually close relatives of pumas
(you know, cougars, or "mountain lions"). So there's no need to bring
African cheetahs to North America to replace an extinct cheetah that was
not even a close relative.

A North American cheetah puts the run on a pronghorn—ensuring that living pronghorn will be the fastest animals in Alberta, thousands of years after the cheetah went extinct.

The Bow Valley at Cochrane

MOST ALBERTANS KNOW that our badlands are one of the richest dinosaur fossil sites on Earth. But how many people realize that Alberta is also home to one of the richest sites for fossil mammals from the time period just after the extinction of the dinosaurs—the Palaeocene Epoch? In the 1920s, pioneer Canadian palaeontologist Loris Russell discovered a deposit of fossil clams, snails and tiny mammal teeth in the banks of the Bow River near the then-tiny ranching town of Cochrane. Since then, the fossils of what we now call the "Cochrane 2" locality have been the subject of intense study at the University of Alberta by Dr. Richard Fox and his students. In fact, I once worked on these fossils myself. The Cochrane fossils might not impress the untrained eye, since they are small and generally fragmentary. But by carefully studying tiny mammal teeth under high magnification, it has become apparent that we have here the remains of a tremendous variety of mammals, most of which were no bigger than a squirrel. And most surprisingly, there is also a fossil from Cochrane of a mammal-like reptile—a group of animals that was thought to have gone extinct some 120 million years earlier. If it were living, we'd call it a "living fossil," but since it already IS a fossil, we call it a "paradox," and thus its full scientific name, *Chronoperates paradoxus.* Not everyone agrees on its identity, but that just gives researchers an excuse to go back to the hillside near Cochrane and look for more evidence one way or the other. I have very fond memories of collecting fossils at Cochrane 2, with the sun glinting off the Bow River, and trains gliding past on the main line of the CPR. It may not be the badlands, but it's still an interesting part of our fossil heritage.

The partial jaws of Chronoperates paradoxus *hover in the air above the Palaeocene-aged rocks along the Bow River near Cochrane.*

Cretaceous Lizards

THERE WAS MORE TO THE AGE OF DINOSAURS than just dinosaurs, and as you probably know it is more commonly referred to as the Age of Reptiles, or the Mesozoic Era. So what kinds of other reptiles were around at the time? I find it fascinating that by about 75 million years ago, not only were there alligators, crocodiles and various quite modern-looking turtles, but there were also members of all of the families of lizards that we find on Earth today. In Alberta, by the way, most of our Mesozoic fossils date from the last period of the Mesozoic Era, the Cretaceous Period, some 65 to 80 million years ago. From the rocks of Dinosaur Provincial Park alone, we have at least six different families of lizards. First, there are the monitor lizards, related to Komodo Dragons and the Australian goannas—big predators. But the teiids were big predators too—relatives of the South American tegus and the American whiptails. Skinks were also present—smooth-scaled lizards with a variety of shapes and lifestyles. And there were anguimorph lizards, related to the living legless and knobby lizards. Finally, the venomous lizards were present here; a group that is now known from only two living members, the Gila Monster of the American Southwest and the Beaded Lizard of the Mexican deserts. There were also members of lizard families that are now extinct, as well as various lizards that are only known from bits and pieces of fossil bone and can't be identified with certainty quite yet. So even though the Late Cretaceous was a time of dinosaurs on the land, pterosaurs in the air, and plesiosaurs in the sea, it was also remarkably modern, if all you looked at were the other reptiles. I doubt that the turtles, crocodilians and lizards would fit any pictures in a modern-day field guide, but they would probably look something like the living species, and many reptiles haven't changed all that much since then. And what about the snakes? Well, that's another story.

An anole, photographed in
Florida—at least some lizards
from the time of the dinosaurs
haven't changed much
since then.

The ancient crocodile *Leidyosuchus* looks a lot like the living American alligator, but not all crocodilians have been this similar over their 200 million-year history.

Alberta's Crocodilians

CROCODILIANS ARE REPTILES and they include crocodiles proper, alligators, and long-snouted Asian things called gharials. We often hear them referred to as "living fossils," and indeed, they haven't changed a whole lot in the last 200 million years. Here in Alberta, during the days of the dinosaurs, there were both crocodiles and alligators and we find their fossils quite commonly in the badlands. Teeth are the most commonly preserved parts of these ancient creatures, but it is also common to find bony scutes—the armour that crocodilians possess, embedded within their skin, at least on the top of the animal. Of course, crocodilians have indeed been evolving all this time—they simply didn't need to evolve too terribly much. Our Late Cretaceous alligator-like animal is called *Albertochampsa*, and although it is something like a living alligator, we now think it represents an extinct branch of the crocodilian family tree. And our most common crocodile, *Leidyosuchus*, was likewise not exactly like any crocodile living today. You know—the more things change, the more they stay the same. During the early history of crocodilian evolution, there were many species that lived on land and had long legs for running. Seagoing crocodilians were also a feature of the Age of Reptiles, with extra-long tails for prolonged swimming. In Madagascar, there was a short-faced plant-eating sort of crocodile. In other words, crocodilians were more diverse back then than they are now. It's a mistake to think of these animals as primitive and unable to change. Instead, they tried out a whole lot of different themes, and settled on a few that worked best. The most incredible fossil crocodile in North America, by the way, was surely *Deinosuchus*. This crocodile had a two-metre skull, and was fully as big as *Tyrannosaurus rex*! In other words, it would have had no trouble eating a dinosaur here and there. *Deinosuchus* is long gone, but remember that when the last dinosaurs became extinct, 65 million years ago, crocodilians survived, peering up from the Alberta swamps, only to drift southward as our climate cooled beyond their ability to tolerate. And speaking of drifting south, *Deinosuchus* never quite made it all the way to Alberta, as far as we know, even in the steamy days of the dinosaurs.

Dawn Redwood Trees

IF YOU VISIT THE CRETACEOUS GARDEN at the Royal Tyrrell Museum, one of the trees you will find growing in this lovely greenhouse is the dawn redwood, *Metasequoia*. Today, there are only about 5,000 living examples of this tree, found in the wild only in the Xiahoe Valley of southeastern China. In the Late Cretaceous, however, *Metasequoia* was found widely in the northern hemisphere and is one of the most common fossil plants in the rocks from which we get our dinosaur bones. The name *Metasequoia* should remind you of sequoia, another name for the group of conifers that includes the giant redwood trees of California, the largest living things on Earth, if you don't count "clones" of poplar trees that are connected by their roots or some giant underground fungus growths (which I don't, since I think the largest living thing should also stand on its own roots, so to speak, even if the fungus is technically larger). *Metasequoia* trees were large, but not as large as the giant sequoia today. In the badlands, it is common not only to find the wood of *Metasequoia*, but also the fine, flat needle-like leaves and the cones. The needles look a bit like balsam fir needles that you can find growing in northern Alberta today, but the needles of *Metasequoia* were arranged in pairs opposite one another on the stem. The cones were almost spherical, much like living sequoia cones but smaller—about the size of a grape. Did the dinosaurs eat *Metasequoia* leaves back in the Late Cretaceous? I doubt it. Today, almost all herbivores feed on the leaves of flowering plants, not conifers. Of course, there are a few insects that specialize on conifer needles, such as spruce budworms, but it still seems likely that the dinosaurs ate other plants. Of course, that doesn't mean they didn't use the dawn redwood forests for shade and for cover. It must have been a wonderful environment, and a lovely place to be, 70-some million years ago in southern Alberta.

The Metasequoia *tree in the Cretaceous Garden of the Royal Tyrrell Museum may not be the centrepiece, but to those who know fossils, it's the star of the show.*

Devil's Coulee and its Dinosaur Nests

IN THE 1880s, geologists visited a place called Fossil Coulee in southern Alberta, near the town of Warner. One of these men was Joseph Burr Tyrrell, the namesake of the Royal Tyrrell Museum. Few fossils of note were recorded and the site was soon overshadowed by the dinosaur-bearing badlands of the Red Deer River valley. In 1987, more than 100 years later, and after Fossil Coulee became known as Devil's Coulee, a teenaged girl named Wendy Sloboda was exploring these same badlands for fossils. She picked up a few pieces of what she thought might be broken eggshell and sent them to Dr. Len Hills of the University of Calgary. In turn, Hills passed the shells along to Dr. Philip Currie of the Royal Tyrrell Museum. Currie sent technicians to Devil's Coulee, and in short order a major discovery was made. As Kevin Aulenback tells it, he was literally speechless when he found not only nearly complete eggs, but also the bones of embryonic dinosaurs that had never hatched. As it turned out, the eggs were laid by duck-billed dinosaurs in a nesting ground along the banks of a river some 75 million years ago. When the waters rose above the banks, the eggs were buried and preserved. Similar eggs and bones had been recently found in Montana as well. The dinosaur in question was given a new name, *Hypacrosaurus stebingeri*, by Phil Currie and his American colleague, Jack Horner of the Museum of the Rockies in Montana. To say that this discovery caused a media sensation would be an understatement. Phil Currie's phone rang incessantly for days on end. For some reason, the idea that giant dinosaurs came from tiny eggs fascinates most people. To palaeontologists, however (and I don't mean to be a party-pooper here!), eggs are exactly what one would expect. The closest relatives of dinosaurs— birds and crocodilians—all lay eggs, and the *real* prize would be a dinosaur showing evidence of live birth. Still, we love our dinosaur eggs and babies, and the town of Warner has set up the Devil's Coulee Dinosaur Heritage Museum to help interpret the story of this historic find in southern Alberta.

Devil's Coulee in southern Alberta—a famous bit of badlands if ever there was one.

Didelphodon, A Sort of Primitive Possum

WHEN MOST PEOPLE THINK OF MARSUPIALS, they think of Australia, and things like kangaroos, koalas, bandicoots, and wombats. There are, however, marsupials closer to home than that, in the form of the Virginia Opossum, a pouched mammal that has never been found in Alberta, but does occur in places like southern Ontario and Quebec. In fact, possum-like marsupials are abundant in Mexico and farther south, although it seems that only in Australia have these fascinating mammals been able to break out of the possum mould. Fossil marsupials are known from Alberta and they date back to the days of the dinosaurs. The split between pouched marsupial mammals and the more familiar placental mammals probably happened not too terribly long before the Cretaceous rocks of our badlands were formed. Cretaceous marsupials are diverse and abundant as fossils, but almost all we know about these animals comes from their teeth. There is a myth about palaeontology, by the way, that a good palaeontologist can reconstruct an entire animal from a single tooth. This is, of course, an exaggeration, but it is based on the amazement that some people feel when they discover that a single tooth can be sufficient to identify the sort of mammal it came from. Cretaceous marsupials in Alberta were, indeed, mostly possum-like, but one, *Didelphodon*, was larger and had teeth adapted for crushing hard shells, much like the teeth of the living sea otter, which feeds on clams and sea urchins. This marsupial also had thickened bones and a paddle-like tail, further evidence that it was semi-aquatic. And what was *Didelphodon* eating? Some have suggested clams, snails, baby turtles, or even baby armoured dinosaurs! Marsupials, of course, survived the extinction at the end of the Cretaceous Period (or they wouldn't be here today), but not without a cost. Some marsupials made it through the event, but most did indeed go extinct. It took a long time for marsupial diversity to recover and it did so most impressively in modern-day Australia and South America, especially when it was separate from North America during the middle of the Age of Mammals.

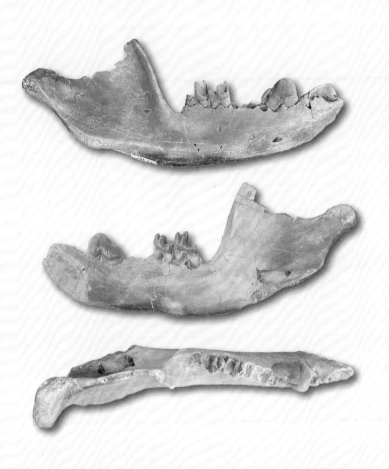

To a trained eye, the lower jaw of Didelphodon gives the impression of strength, with powerful crushing teeth.

The badlands of Dinosaur Provincial Park are vast enough that entire fossil bones can weather out of the hills undetected and erode away to nothing before they are discovered.

Dinosaur Provincial Park

Dinosaur Provincial Park contains the largest patch of badland topography in southern Alberta and the semi-desert landscape is a marvel to behold, what with its cacti, rattlesnakes and other reminders of the American Southwest. Many of the dinosaur specimens in the Royal Tyrrell Museum, as well as in other museums around the world, come from Dinosaur Provincial Park. As you visit museums outside of Alberta, watch for names like Steveville, Deadlodge Canyon and Little Sandhill Creek, the old names for the area that is now the park. The prominence of these fossils is a large part of the reason the park was made a World Heritage Site by UNESCO in 1979, long after the park was founded in 1955. Today, the park is home to the Field Station of the Royal Tyrrell Museum, as well as a lovely campground and a fine system of trails and exhibits. This is likely the best window we have on the time period 73 to 76 million years ago, although there are sites of equivalent age in Montana, Utah, China and Mongolia. The park has so far produced over 500 partial to complete dinosaur skeletons, from some 35 species of dinosaur. Such names as *Styracosaurus, Centrosaurus, Albertosaurus, Troodon* and *Lambeosaurus* are all dinosaurs from the park. As well, the park has produced fossils of turtles, crocodilians, fishes, clams and champsosaurs. Oddly, however, it has not produced many fossils of large plants (although it does produce pollen—one of the best pollen records anywhere) or the fossils of many invertebrates other than clams and snails. When the rocks of the Dinosaur Park Formation were laid down, rivers flowed from the west, from volcanic hills long before the Rocky Mountains were formed. These rivers emptied into the Bearpaw Sea, forming deltas, lakes, lagoons and riverbank deposits. Now, we see the sandstones, mudstones and coal beds that these deposits have become. In the Cretaceous Period, the climate was seasonal but not cold—sort of like Florida today. The dinosaur rush of the early 20th century was centred here, with such famous fossil hunters as the Sternbergs and Barnum Brown scouring the ever-eroding badlands for dinosaur remains. Since then, the fossils of the park have been studied by palaeontologists at the University of Alberta, the Provincial Museum of Alberta (now the Royal Alberta Museum) and the Royal Tyrrell Museum, which opened in 1985.

Dromaeosaurus, A Snappy Little Raptor

AMONG DINOSAUR ENTHUSIASTS, the phrase "small theropod" has a
magical quality to it. Alberta's best-known palaeontologist, Dr. Phil Currie,
has spent most of his career studying small theropods. But what on earth
is a theropod, and if they were dinosaurs, why aren't we more interested in
the large theropods? Well, to begin with, theropods were meat-eating dinosaurs and just about every meat-eating dinosaur that ever lived falls in the
theropod group. They were generally bipedal, with sharp teeth and strong
hind legs. The biggest theropods, like *Tyrannosaurus*, are reasonably well
understood. But the small theropods are not only more diverse, they are
also more of a challenge, in part because most are known only from partial
skeletons and fragmentary fossils. One of the best known of Alberta's small
theropods is a dinosaur named *Dromaeosaurus*. This was a two-metre long
creature at best, and a fairly typical member of its group, with a long tail,
grasping hands, sharp teeth and claws, and an upright slashing claw on one
of the toes of its hind foot. If you visit the Field Station of the Royal Tyrrell
Museum in Dinosaur Provincial Park near Brooks, you will see a wonderful
display in which the skeletons of three *Dromaeosaurus* are mounted in lifelike positions, surrounding a much larger duck-billed dinosaur in a very
menacing way. The idea that small theropods hunted in packs first originated with a slightly larger relative, *Deinonychus*, from the western United
States. When the bones of many *Deinonychus* were found together, palaeontologists suspected that perhaps they had been social animals, hunting
in groups. Is this a stretch, or is it reasonable to suggest that theropods
could hunt their prey the way much more intelligent wolves do today? Well,
in my opinion it's not much of a stretch at all. There is one species of North
American hawk, the Harris's Hawk, that hunts in groups and is not much
brainier than a theropod. However, just because bones are buried together
doesn't mean that the animals they belonged to lived together, and this
may be one of those things that we never really know for sure.

The skeleton of Dromaeosaurus hunkers over its skeletal prey. We get used to seeing dinosaur skeletons in lifelike poses, and then adding flesh, skin and sparkling eyes in our imagination.

The Drumheller Badlands

THE MOST FAMOUS DINOSAUR FOSSIL LOCALITY in Alberta is, of course, Drumheller—at least among the general population. Ask a palae-ontologist and she or he will probably give you a different answer, such as Dinosaur Provincial Park, near Brooks. That's because the badlands near Drumheller (in what we call the Horseshoe Canyon and Scollard Formations of rock) are many millions of years younger than those farther downstream along the Red Deer River (in what we call the Oldman and Dinosaur Park Formations). By the time the Drumheller badlands rocks had been deposited, the number of different types of dinosaurs in Alberta had actually decreased. Whereas Dinosaur Provincial Park has produced some 35 species of dinosaur, the Drumheller Badlands have produced only about 25 species (which is still, of course, A LOT of dinosaurs). This intriguing bit of evidence has led some palaeontologists to wonder if the extinction of the dinosaurs was perhaps a gradual process and not simply the result of a meteorite impact 65 million years ago. Perhaps the dinosaurs were

already in decline when the meteorite hit. So why is Drumheller so wonderfully famous if the best dinosaurs are elsewhere? It has a lot to do with the town's long-time promotion of dinosaur tourism, which replaced coal mining as the main industry somewhere around the time that I was born in the late 1950s. So when the province decided to build what is now the Royal Tyrrell Museum, Drumheller was the obvious place to do it. And as a consequence, with all of the palaeontologists at the Museum, we now know more about the dinosaurs of Drumheller than we ever did before, with new discoveries in the past few years of such things as *Edmontosaurus*, *Troodon* and *Albertosaurus*. As well, if we look back to the great Canadian dinosaur rush from 1910 to 1916, Drumheller was the first place that fossil hunters such as Barnum Brown and the Sternbergs came to hunt for dinosaur bones. So, even if Drumheller doesn't have as many dinosaurs as Dinosaur Provincial Park, it's still one of the finest dinosaur locations on Earth and one of the biggest tourist attractions in Alberta.

The town of Drumheller as photographed by George Sternberg in 1916. Back then, Drumheller was blissfully unaware of the fossiliferous fame that would one day fuel its economy.

Dry Island Buffalo Jump Provincial Park

APART FROM HAVING THE LONGEST NAME of any provincial park in
Alberta, this magnificent expanse of badlands is also a phenomenal location for the fossils of dinosaurs and other extinct animals from the Late
Cretaceous, near the end of the Age of Reptiles. Dry Island Buffalo Jump is
located north and west of Drumheller, about halfway to Red Deer, along the
Red Deer River near the town of Elnora. As you approach it from any direction, road signs will guide you in. This is a day-use park and no camping or
overnight stays are allowed. For this reason, Dry Island is a largely undis-
covered wonderland. The poplar-lined banks of the Red Deer River lead
up into a huge expanse of richly-coloured badlands and the badlands
are far enough north to have small patches of spruce trees on some of
their north-facing slopes—something you rarely, if ever, see in the better
known badlands farther south. Beginning in the early 1900s, fossil hunters
became aware of the rich fossil treasures of this area and palaeontologists
from the Royal Tyrrell Museum are still finding much to excavate there
today. Among other finds, a huge *Triceratops* dinosaur skull has recently
been excavated. The most famous fossils from this site, however, are the
jumbled bones of *Albertosaurus*, the smaller near relative of *Tyrannosaurus*.
Phil Currie from the University of Alberta and a research associate of the
Royal Tyrrell Museum are collaborating with other palaeontologists to see
if this "*Albertosaurus* bonebed" can tell us about whether these meat-eating
dinosaurs lived together (as well as being fossilized together), and what
bones of different sizes can tell us about the growth of *Albertosaurus* from
partly grown young to adulthood. Why "Dry Island?" Well, in the middle of
the badlands, there is a forested hill that is still almost as high as the prairies surrounding the badlands—this is the "dry island." And why "buffalo
jump"? Native people once stampeded bison over a high cliff on the west
side of the badlands and collected the meat and hides at the bottom. It all
makes sense. Perhaps the name could be made even longer—how about
"Dry Island Buffalo Jump, Dinosaur Fossil, *Albertosaurus* Bonebed, and
Badlands Vista Provincial Park?"

Top: The sandstone formations at Dry Island are as spectacular as any in Alberta. Bottom: A crew
works on the Albertosaurus bonebed, while a plaster-jacketed bone awaits transport to the museum.

Dunkleosteus, A Very Scary Fish

LONG BEFORE THE AGE OF REPTILES, the world was living in what we now think of as the Age of Fishes, the Devonian Period, about 350 million years ago. Just about the time the first amphibians were taking to the land, the seas were teeming with great reef communities, built around reef-building sponges, not corals as we know today. The fish diversity was impressive and it included sharks, bony fishes, jawless fishes and, most importantly, placoderms. So what's a placoderm? Sounds like something a dentist would say, doesn't it? Well, "placoderm" means "plated skin" and it refers to the fact that the outer surface of these fish was covered in large bony plates that were used for protection. Most placoderms were small or medium-sized, but one grew very, very large. This was *Dunkleosteus*. *Dunkleosteus* was about 10 metres long, full grown—that's a big fish. And the front end of its body was completely armoured in bony plates, despite the fact that it was the biggest carnivore around in its day—the biggest animal period, in fact. *Dunkleosteus* even had a ring of bony plates around its eye, protecting the eye from accidental damage, and instead of teeth the mouth of *Dunkleosteus* was lined with huge cutting plates of bone ("dermal bone" as we call it). Jaws were a relatively new evolutionary development during those days and not everyone had teeth. These monsters probably ate sharks, and hey, if you eat sharks you earn the right to be called a monster. Visitors to the Royal Tyrrell Museum will remember the skull of *Dunkleosteus* that stands at the top of the stairs before you descend to the Dinosaur Hall. It is a popular exhibit and these cast bones come from a famous specimen discovered in Ohio. I find it exciting to know that fossils of *Dunkleosteus* have also been found in Alberta. In fact, I've seen one of the cutting plates from a *Dunkleosteus* jaw that was picked up in a gravel pit near Canmore. To me, that plate is as scary as a *Tyrannosaurus* tooth.

Dunkleosteus—*the creature that holds the title of "Scariest Toothless Face in the History of Our Planet."*

Edmonton, A Modest Sort of Dinosaur Graveyard

THE RIVER VALLEY in Edmonton seems far from the badlands of southern Alberta and not at all like a dinosaur graveyard. Yet much of the rock in the Edmonton area dates from the end of the Age of Dinosaurs and some of it even contains fossils. If you look at any of the high cliffs along the valley of the North Saskatchewan River (for example, the area across from Fort Edmonton) you can clearly see two colours in the rocks. At the top of the hill, the rock is light brown. This is the clay sediment from the bottom of Glacial Lake Edmonton that covered the entire Edmonton area when the last glaciers melted away. If you ignore the river valley, the Edmonton region is really quite flat, and that is because 10,000 years ago we were at the bottom of the lake. Below the brown rock the colour turns to grey. This is the Late Cretaceous sandstone and siltstone that we call the Wapiti Formation north of the river and the Horseshoe Canyon Formation south of the river. And yes, these rocks do contain the remains of dinosaurs. A few partial duck-billed dinosaur skeletons have been excavated in and around Edmonton, and even the casual prospector can expect to find fragments of bone, as well as the occasional dinosaur tooth, clam shell, or piece of petrified wood. That's about all I have ever found there myself. The dinosaur-bearing rocks are mostly sandstone, and sandstone is generally created in fast-flowing rivers, in which the current carries away smaller silt and clay particles, leaving only the sand behind. That also means that any bones or dinosaur carcasses would have been tumbled along the bottom, broken into pieces, and weathered by the current. In fact, that's exactly what you see when you find a decent-sized piece of dinosaur bone in Edmonton. And of course, please remember that excavating a fossil, even with a pointy stick or jack-knife, is not legal without a permit. If you find something interesting, please contact the Royal Tyrrell Museum.

The river valley in Edmonton, with rocks the same age as those in Drumheller.

Edmontosaurus, *the duck-billed dinosaur. In many ways, it was much like the moose that we see in this area today, albeit naked and with a huge tail!*

Edmontosaurus, **Edmonton's Duck-billed Dinosaur**

WHEN ALBERTANS THINK OF DINOSAURS they think of Drumheller, but one of the most common dinosaurs in North America was indirectly named after the city of Edmonton. *Edmontosaurus* was a huge, 13-metre long, 4-tonne duck-billed dinosaur and it was originally discovered in southern Alberta, in rocks that were then called the Edmonton Beds, named for the city of Edmonton much farther north. The names of the rocks have been changed, but the name of the dinosaur has stayed the same. *Edmontosaurus* should perhaps have been called "Drumhellerosaurus," but in science the names of animals don't have to make perfect sense, they just have to serve as standard labels for particular groups and species. It is worth noting, however, that fossils that may well have come from *Edmontosaurus* have indeed been found within the city limits of Edmonton. The man who, in 1917, named *Edmontosaurus* was Lawrence Lambe, and Lambe in turn had another duck-billed dinosaur named in his honour, *Lambeosaurus*. *Lambeosaurus* had a crest on its head; *Edmontosaurus* did not. The fossil collections of the Royal Tyrrell Museum include many *Edmontosaurus* specimens, including a skull that was found only a few kilometres from the Museum. Unfortunately for us, however, the most famous *Edmontosaurus* fossils were discovered not in Alberta, but in Kansas in 1908 and 1910, and are now in New York and in Frankfurt, Germany. These were the famous dinosaur "mummies," in which fossilized skin impressions were found covering the bones of their skeletons. When Charles H. Sternberg, the legendary fossil hunter, saw the first of these mummies and realized that it was his son George who found it, he exclaimed: "George, this is a finer fossil than I have ever found, and the only thing that would have given me greater pleasure would have been to have discovered it myself." A proud father, a proud son and a "mummy" that certainly deserved to be the object of such pride.

Edmontonia, Edmonton's Other Dinosaur

As an Edmontonian, I'd like to take pride in both of the dinosaur names that bear the city's name: *Edmontosaurus* and *Edmontonia*. But as a scientist, I know that would be cheating. Both dinosaurs were named for the rocks in which they were found, rocks that were once called the "Edmonton Beds" and that extended all the way from Edmonton (where they were named) south to the badlands of the Red Deer River. These rocks were laid down near the end of the Age of Reptiles, in what we call the Late Cretaceous times. While *Edmontosaurus* was a duck-billed dinosaur, and a fairly common fossil, *Edmontonia* was an armoured dinosaur and is not very well known by comparison, although it is still one of the best-known armoured dinosaurs of all. *Edmontonia* was a four-legged plant eater, about seven metres long and weighed about as much as a bison. It was covered in small plates of bony armour, set right into the skin of its back, and the skull of this dinosaur was also heavily armoured. It was a member of the family Nodosauridae, and as such it had a simple, pointed tail. The other family of armoured dinosaurs, the Ankylosauridae, includes the larger armoured dinosaurs with bony clubs on their tail. Don't get the impression that *Edmontonia* didn't have cool anatomical weapons, though. Jutting out of its shoulders were four huge, pointed spikes that protected its shoulder region very nicely, I'm sure. *Edmontonia* was named in 1928 by Charlie Sternberg, a central figure in early Alberta palaeontology, on the basis of fossils he found in southern Alberta. I find it interesting that the American palaeontologist, Bob Bakker, named another species of armoured dinosaur in Charlie Sternberg's honour, *Chassternbergia*, only to discover later that the fossils really belonged to *Edmontonia*, the dinosaur Sternberg named in the first place. Either way, the Sternberg legacy is preserved and science marches on. These sorts of mistakes are inevitable when we deal with fragmentary fossils of long-dead creatures, and to be honest, it's the challenge that fuels much of the enthusiasm that dinosaur palaeontologists have for their work. Having said this, however, recent work by Matt Vickaryous has suggested that *Edmontonia* may not be distinguishable from the related dinosaur *Panoplosaurus*. If they prove to be the same thing, the name *Panoplosaurus* is older and would therefore replace *Edmontonia*, leaving Edmonton with only one namesake dinosaur.

Edmontonia

This was one of the most common armoured dinosaurs in Alberta. Large and well protected, it had small teeth and weak jaws. Unlike some of its close relatives, it lacked a tail club and had spines only around its neck and shoulders.

Edmontonia, as a reconstructed model—certainly one of the best-armoured animals ever to exist.

Feathered Dinosaurs

WHAT DID YOU DO FOR YOUR SUMMER VACATION? In 2005, my wife and I travelled to London and New York, where we visited, respectively, the Natural History Museum and the American Museum of Natural History—both with Alberta dinosaurs collected 90-some years ago on display. But the big news on both continents is the relatively recent discovery of small, feathered bird-like dinosaurs in a place called Liaoning in China. These fossils not only show the link between dinosaurs and birds, they also demonstrate that dinosaurs probably had feathers first. So why don't we have feathered dinosaur fossils here in Alberta? Well, no one believes that all the big, scary dinosaurs lived here while all the small fluffy dinosaurs lived in China. Instead, there were differences in the conditions for fossilization—the fine shales of Liaoning were great for preserving small-bodied animals and the details of their feathers. The rivers and deltas of Cretaceous Alberta were better for preserving the bones of large animals, often as complete or nearly complete skeletons. The bones of small creatures are found here, but usually scattered here and there, and never in rocks that can preserve the fine details of such things as feathers or hair. As I looked at the Liaoning fossils (the originals of which were on tour here in Alberta a few years ago, by the way) I wondered how dinosaur science would have been different if the Liaoning fossils had been discovered first, if we didn't know about the giant Jurassic dinosaurs from the US, and we were just now uncovering the riches of the Alberta badlands. Perhaps the headlines would read something like "New discoveries in Alberta prove that the Cretaceous Period was populated not only by small, normal-looking bird-like creatures, but also by a tremendous variety of gigantic, fantastic-looking dinosaurs unlike anything ever seen before. Horned dinosaurs, crested dinosaurs with duck-like bills and the biggest meat eater that ever lived, a thing called *Tyrannosaurus*." Of course, it didn't happen this way, but in palaeontology the order in which things are discovered can have a tremendous impact on how we think about them.

Caudipteryx, *a Chinese feathered dinosaur, looking for all the world like a turkey's worst Halloween nightmare.*

Fossil Frogs

FROGS ARE AMPHIBIANS, but the first amphibians to crawl out of the water 370 million years ago during the Devonian Period were not frogs. Frogs did not appear for another 170 million years, at about the same time as the first dinosaurs and the first mammals. Clearly, it's a mistake to think of them as "primitive" creatures. By the time fossil frogs start to show up in good numbers in the Cretaceous rocks of Alberta, frogs had been around for about ²/₃ of their time on Earth. If we could travel back to the Cretaceous Period and wander among the dinosaurs (in what was then a coastal lowland, and is now the badlands of southern Alberta), we would see frogs. Not only that, we would see frogs that look a lot like those living today. Today, there are about 30 different families of frogs on Earth and the majority of these general sorts of frogs had evolved by the end of dinosaurian times. There were no toads, in the modern sense, and there were no tree frogs, but most other sorts of frogs were there. Some were aquatic and had no tongue, like the living clawed frogs of Africa and the Suriname Toads of South America. At least we assume they had no tongue—there is no such thing as a fossilized tongue that I know of. And some were semi-terrestrial, hopping around on land and catching bugs with their sticky tongues, in typical frog fashion. Like living frogs, Cretaceous frogs undoubtedly spent their early life as tadpoles, but if you think finding fossil frogs is tough, believe me when I say that fossil tadpoles (with very few bones or other hardened structures in their bodies) are even more rare. The skeletons of adult frogs break apart easily after death, and thus the study of fossil frogs is often the study of isolated bones. At the Royal Tyrrell Museum, the collections manager, Jim Gardner, studies fossil frogs and finds them wonderfully challenging. Jim has also studied fossil tadpoles from sediments in the western United States, but so far he hasn't found any here in Alberta.

Fire-bellied toads (in the family Discoglossidae), a familiar sort of pet store animal from Asia, would not have seemed out of place during the dinosaur times in Alberta.

Heavy scales and fan-like tails: a group of fossil Lepisosteus *gar on a boulder from the west end of Calgary.*

Gar, The Fish

ONE OF THE MOST COMMON TYPES of fish fossil in Alberta is the gar scale. In many of our badlands, it is typical for some places to be literally strewn with the diamond-shaped bony scales of this marvellous fish. These familiar fossils look a bit like angular black pumpkin seeds. Scales of this sort are typical of the so-called primitive fishes, as opposed to the thin-scaled fish we are more familiar with today. In any event, gar are a sort of long, thin, pike-like predatory fish and they also form a great connection between the present and the past. There are, in fact, five species of gar living in the southeastern US today, especially in rivers flowing into the Gulf of Mexico, which as we know was once the Bearpaw Sea that covered much of eastern Alberta during the last part of the Age of Dinosaurs. The five species include the long-nosed gar, short-nosed gar, spotted gar, Florida gar and alligator gar. As far as fossil gar are concerned, our best Albertan specimens are now part of a big study of gar centred at the Field Museum in Chicago. Most people are unclear on what a gar really is, and I can't blame them. Gar are often called "gar pike" but gar are only superficially similar to pike, the fish most Albertans call the jackfish. Both, however, are designed for high-speed ambush attacks on their prey. Gar, like pike, cruise slowly through the water, often under the cover of weeds, and then with a quick surge of muscular power through their long narrow bodies, they dart forward and grasp their prey in their long toothy jaws. The name "alligator gar" has a great sound to it and as a result it has been applied here and there to many fish other than the true alligator gar of the southeast. And of course these fish are in no way closely related to alligators. In pet stores, a wide variety of long-bodied predatory fish are sold as "gar," "gar pike," or "alligator gar," and some of them actually are gar, by gar. Others are simply gar-like, but pet stores do not sell pike or pike-relatives. This tells you that the gar-style body plan is common among fish. And yes, keeping a pet gar is like having a bit of the Cretaceous Period in your living room and if you have a big enough tank and you don't feel sorry for the so-called "feeder goldfish" that go along with gar ownership, you might find a pet gar to be just the thing. Of course, you can always visit the Royal Tyrrell Museum to admire both the fossil and the living gar—but I'll leave that up to you.

Horn Corals

IN THE ROCKY MOUNTAINS OF ALBERTA, it's hard to find a dinosaur fossil. Other sorts of fossils, however, can be quite abundant. For mountain hikers, one of the most common finds is a thing called a horn coral, so named because each fossil is about the size and shape of a small sheep or goat horn. They are tapered to a blunt point, clearly made from stacks of thin rings, and quite rough and bumpy-looking as well. They date from a time long before the dinosaurs—the Palaeozoic Era, when most of the Alberta oil was being formed—and are common in Devonian rocks. Horn corals, or at least most horn corals, did not form reefs the way many corals do today in the warmer tropical seas. Most horn corals were solitary creatures, and were not well anchored to the sea bottom. Since Alberta is far from the ocean, readers can be forgiven for not knowing exactly what a coral is. Corals are the skeletons of small animals related to jellyfish, hydras and sea anemones. The coral polyp, as it is called, secretes the hard skeleton around it, and lives inside, poking its tentacles out and upward to feed on passing small creatures and other bits of food. Picture a sea anemone—those many-tentacled and often colourful soft-bodied animals that look like a cross between a flower and an octopus, living in a hardened tube of calcite crystals. A better name for horn corals is rugose corals, since many sorts of coral living today also have the word horn in their name. And if you are wondering if there is anything truly interesting about horn corals, my own favourite story is that the daily growth rings in horn corals have been used to calculate the length of the Palaeozoic year, at about 400 days. If you and I had been fortunate enough to be born as horn corals, we'd have so much more time to get things done. But for a horn coral, I suspect, one day was much like the next, and very few tasks were truly urgent.

Horn coral fossils of the general sort that have been used to calculate the lazy 400-day years of Palaeozoic times.

How Do You Know Where To Dig?

"How do you know where to dig?" That is probably the most commonly asked question in all of palaeontology, except perhaps for "if they all had a fight, which dinosaur would win?" And like all common questions, it is common for the simple reason that the answer is not at all what people expect it to be. The fact is, palaeontologists who search for large fossils generally *don't* know where to dig! And except in rare instances, the digging never precedes the discovery. Instead, palaeontologists prospect for fossils the way gold hunters prospect for gold. They go to eroded places such as badlands, riverbanks and road cuts, and they first search for the right kinds of rocks. Once they find what looks like a promising spot, the search begins—sometimes at a quick walk, but more often in a stoop, or even on hands and knees. And if you think the goal is to find an entire skeleton stretched out on the ground before you, you're wrong. When that happens, it is usually cause for tears, not celebration, since the fossils are likely to have been ruined by the elements by the time they are entirely exposed by erosion. No, instead, we look for just the smallest bit of a fossil protruding from the ground. With luck, a small bit of bone will alert the scientist to a much larger find still that is protected by the surrounding rock, and when that happens the next step is to clear away huge amounts of rock and carefully prepare the fossil for transport back to the lab. It sometimes takes years before the process of uncovering a fossil is complete. And yes, this is the reason why it is important to leave all fossils where you find them—in case they are the clue that leads to a big discovery. This is also why it is illegal to excavate fossils in Alberta without a permit. There are, however, some sorts of palaeontology that do rely on a "dig first, ask questions later" approach. For example, the study of fossil pollen and other small fossils is often a matter of processing rock in search of tiny treasures. And for fossils on shale, we generally sit with a hammer and a chisel and split pieces of shale in the hope that we will uncover a fine flattened find. Basically, it's as much about hard work as knowing where to dig.

Two views of a typical dinosaur quarry that probably began with the discovery of a tiny bit of bone protruding through the surface into the sunlight.

Hypacrosaurus, Less than the Ultimate Dinosaur

DUCK-BILLED DINOSAURS were apparently the most abundant dinosaurs in ancient Alberta and *Hypacrosaurus* was a duck-billed dinosaur. Personally, I never paid it any attention at all until its eggs were discovered at Devil's Coulee in southern Alberta in the late 1980s. So let's spend a few moments with *Hypacrosaurus* now, and I'll give it the attention it deserves. *Hypacrosaurus* was formally named and described by the American fossil hunter and palaeontologist Barnum Brown in 1913. He called it *Hypacrosaurus altispinus*, a name that means something like "high-spined, below the top lizard." I'll come back to the "below the top" bit momentarily, but I do understand "high-spined," or *altispinus*. One of the things that distinguishes *Hypacrosaurus* fossils are their very high neural spines—the bony crests that stick up from the tops of the vertebrae, or back bones. These are what you feel when you run your fingers up or down your own backbone, or that of someone near and dear to you. On *Hypacrosaurus*, they were huge, and they look like those of a bison. On a bison, they support the great hump on the animal's back and this was probably the case with *Hypacrosaurus* as well. The skull of *Hypacrosaurus* was also top-heavy and it bore a rounded hollow crest. This crest was smaller than that of some of *Hypacrosaurus*'s close relatives, and perhaps this is what makes *Hypacrosaurus* something that is below the top, in the sense of "not quite the ultimate." Others have suggested that Barnum Brown was impressed by the great size of *Hypacrosaurus* and named it such in comparison to *Tyrannosaurus*, the greatest so-called "lizard" of them all. But while *Tyrannosaurus* reached 14 metres in length and weighed six tonnes, *Hypacrosaurus* measured a mere nine metres in length and weighed only four tonnes. *Hypacrosaurus altispinus* is known from the Horseshoe Canyon Formation of rocks near Drumheller and lived near the end of the Age of Dinosaurs. The other species of *Hypacrosaurus*, *Hypacrosaurus stebingeri*, is known from rocks farther south and is the one that left its eggs at Devil's Coulee. It lived almost 10 million years earlier. They both may have been "less than the ultimate" among dinosaurs, but they were still wondrous, successful creatures in their day.

Hypacrosaurus altispinus *on display at the Royal Tyrrell Museum, in what is called a "panel mount."*

The Kleskun Hills

WHEN ALBERTANS THINK OF BADLANDS, they generally think Drumheller, or possibly Dinosaur Provincial Park near Brooks. Some of us have also experienced the scenic badlands along the South Saskatchewan River and the Milk River, even farther south. Badlands are formed by erosion and, in particular, erosion of soft bedrock by water. In dry places, where plants have a hard time establishing themselves on rapidly eroding slopes, the result is badlands—so named because they are bad for travel, especially on horseback or with covered wagons. One of Alberta's most interesting patches of badlands is also one of the farthest north—the Kleskun Hills, 20 km east of Grande Prairie. There, the dry climate of the Peace River grasslands keeps the forest at bay and a large expanse of Late Cretaceous rock has eroded into a perfectly typical patch of badlands, complete with the occasional dinosaur fossil. Kleskun Hill Park gives easy public access to the site, and it's certainly worth a visit on your own personal tour of Alberta's scenic hotspots. It is also one of the last remaining undisturbed portions of the Peace River grasslands and is home to a number of unique butterflies, now under study at the University of Alberta. A few years back, my long-time friend Margot Hervieux (who also studied the Peace River butterflies) invited me to the Kleskun Hills to revive a tradition called the "geology picnic" after a 40-year hiatus. In the old days, palaeontologists such as Charlie Sternberg used to give public lectures in the hills at an event that apparently emphasized community spirit, family values and the need for better public understanding of the sedimentary geology of the area. I dressed up as Sternberg for the re-enactment, and after studying a 1978 film about Sternberg, I was pretty good at imitating him. In the film, produced by the National Film Board of Canada, my favourite moment came when the 96-year-old Charlie said "If I had my life to live over, I'd be a...dinosaur expert!" And hey, so would I!

A bit of typical dinosaur-aged rock in the Kleskun Hills of northern Alberta, many hours' drive north of the closest similar landform.

Lambeosaurus, Lambe's Dinosaur

THE NAME *LAMBEOSAURUS*, which refers to a sort of duck-billed dinosaur, makes more sense if you pronounce it Lambe-o-saurus, since this
genus of dinosaurs was named for Lawrence Lambe, an early palaeontologist. Lambe worked for the Geological Survey of Canada, beginning in
1897, and he is responsible for the names of many of our familiar dinosaurs, including *Edmontosaurus* and *Styracosaurus*. It is fitting, then, that
in 1923 William Parks named a duck-billed dinosaur in Lambe's honour—
Lambeosaurus lambei. Parks was another early Canadian palaeontologist,
who in turn was the namesake of *Parksosaurus,* another dinosaur discussed
in this book. If you look at fossils or pictures of *Lambeosaurus,* you will
quickly realize that there are two types of *Lambeosaurus: Lambeosaurus
lambei,* with a low crest over the forehead and a backward-projecting
fingerlike crest behind it, and *Lambeosaurus magnacristatus,* with a great
helmet-shaped, forward-sweeping crest. *Magnacristatus,* by the way, means
"great crested." Many newcomers to dinosaur science wonder at first why
these two rather dissimilar-looking creatures share the same name, but
the details of the rest of these dinosaurs' skeletons make it clear that they
are close relatives, differing mainly in the shapes of their heads. Often,
such differences are used to justify giving each different-looking dinosaur
a different genus name, but in my opinion it is wise to use these names to
group related species together. Besides, it means fewer names to memo-
rize. When I was young, the best dinosaur skeleton at the Provincial
Museum of Alberta (which is now, of course, the Royal Alberta Museum)
was a *Lambeosaurus magnacristatus* mounted on a flat panel of sand in
the position in which the skeleton had been found. I clearly remember
standing alone in the gallery, looking at the skeleton while a whirring
security camera panned over to check on me. There was a moment there
when I realized, suddenly, just how tremendously old the bones in front of
me were, and that they were indeed the remains of a gigantic monstrous
animal, forever gone from the Earth. That moment, and that feeling, have
been with me ever since.

A very fine portrait of palaeontologist Lawrence Lambe and the dinosaur that twice bears his
surname, Lambeosaurus lambei.

The skull of Leptoceratops in side view. The large sand-filled opening near the centre at the top is where the eye would have been.

Leptoceratops, A Hornless Horned Dinosaur

LEPTOCERATOPS is one of Alberta's least-known dinosaurs, but that is
a shame, since it is also one of the most interesting. *Leptoceratops* was a
small, two-metre long plant-eating dinosaur that was related to the big-
horned dinosaurs such as *Triceratops*. Like them, it had a large head, a
beak as well as chewing teeth in its mouth, and a bony frill to protect the
neck. Its name means "slender-horned face," but unlike its larger relatives,
Leptoceratops had no horns. The American palaeontologist Barnum Brown
discovered *Leptoceratops* in 1910. The first *Leptoceratops* fossils were found
in the badlands of the Red Deer River near the town of Rumsey, Alberta.
Part of the skeleton had eroded away and the remaining bones that were
exposed on the surface had been trampled by cattle. Still, there were
enough good bones in the rock to make it a wonderful discovery of not one
but two skeletons of this dinosaur. A second specimen of *Leptoceratops* was
discovered and excavated by Charles M. Sternberg in the late 1940s, also
from the badlands of the Red Deer River north and west of Drumheller.
Since then more fossils of these animals have emerged, including a Royal
Tyrrell Museum find of an older and distinctive jaw bone from the badlands
of Dinosaur Provincial Park and two more partial skeletons from the area
north of Drumheller. Now if you're thinking, "Hey, this dinosaur sounds
like it was a lot like *Protoceratops*, the famous hornless horned dinosaur
from Mongolia," you are right—they were closely related. In fact, we think
that Western North America and Asia were connected for at least part
of the Cretaceous Period, across what is now the Bering Strait between
Siberia and Alaska. So it's not surprising to find similar dinosaurs from that
time period on both continents. What is surprising is that the big-horned
dinosaurs, such as *Triceratops*, only lived here and are unknown as fossils
in Asia, except for a few tantalizing bits. Was the environment there not
to their liking? Were they unable to cross the land connection? Are their
fossils still waiting to be discovered in Asia? Perhaps we'll never know, but
this is one of many mysteries that keep palaeontology a vibrant science.

Alberta's Lions

WHAT WOULD AFRICA BE without prides of lions roaming the Serengeti Plains and feasting on the abundant herds of grazing animals that share their savannah home? Well, it would be like Alberta. Before the end of the Ice Age, about 10,000 years ago, there were many more species of large mammals in North America, including mammoths, mastodons, giant ground sloths, short-faced bears and, yes, lions. The North American lion, *Panthera atrox*, was, as far as we can tell, almost identical to the living African lion, but just a wee bit bigger. I have seen part of a lion skull unearthed near Lethbridge, and next to the skull of a very large Bengal Tiger, the lion fossil was bigger. Lion and tiger bones are extremely similar, by the way, and it is worth noting that from the bones alone we would never guess that lions are highly social and live in prides, while tigers are loners outside of the breeding season. So we don't really know if the North American lion was a social animal or not. We also don't know for sure if the males had manes, the way living lions do. To a palaeontologist, 10,000 years ago is just yesterday, and that is not simply a matter of palaeontologists being a bit jaded on such matters. Certainly, the first people in North America had to contend with lions. But like the lions themselves, the first people would have found themselves in the midst of a tremendous abundance of large, potentially edible, mammals. Hunting must have been quite easy, if hunting large mammals with simple weapons is ever truly "easy." Some people have suggested that the disappearance of most of the large mammals that lived here at the end of the Ice Age was the result of overhunting by early people, but others think that climate change and subsequent changes in vegetation were to blame. Either way, two things are clear: there is no lion safari industry in Alberta, and ranchers have one less thing to worry about.

The lions that once roamed near Lethbridge were probably a lot like African lions, but it is reasonable to suggest that they lacked manes, like living lionesses and cubs.

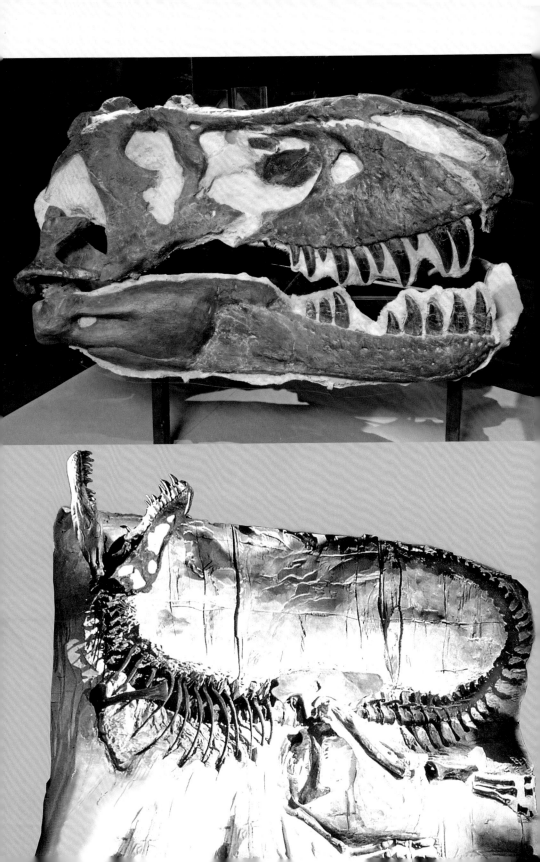

Lundbreck Falls and the Black Beauty

TYRANNOSAURUS are not only the most famous dinosaurs that ever lived; some of them even have names. Perhaps you've heard of "Sue," the *T. rex* from South Dakota that is now the feature exhibit at Chicago's Field Museum? Sue is billed as the largest and most complete *T. rex* ever, and she was also at the centre of a huge legal battle before Sotheby's sold her to the Field Museum for $8.4 million dollars. Quite a story! But Alberta also has a *T. rex* with a nickname, the Black Beauty. I know—that's also a horse's name, but hey, it works for me. Black Beauty was discovered in the lower part of the Crowsnest Pass in Alberta, near Lundbreck Falls. As *Tyrannosaurus* go the specimen is about average in size, but to be honest, it really is beautiful. Black Beauty was preserved in very hard, light grey sandstone, but the bones and teeth of this tremendous meat eater are shining black—stained during fossilization by minerals. Because the rock was so hard, getting the fossil out of the ground was not easy. In technician Darren Tanke's words, "it was a real he-man type of quarry." I believe it. In 1980, I was working for Dr. Phil Currie and spent part of my time on one single toe bone from the Black Beauty specimen. After chipping away at the immensely hard sandstone for two weeks, one blow of the chisel finally separated all the rock from the bone, and the job was done. But it took thousands and thousands of blows before that happened. Alberta's other *T. rex* came from near the town of Huxley, but I don't think it has a nickname. To the south in Montana, the Museum of the Rockies in Bozeman named their *T. rex* "B. rex," after technician Bob Harmon, and B. rex was in the news not long ago. South Carolina palaeontologist Mary Schweitzer discovered evidence that B. rex was a girl, based on the presence of medullary tissue lining the bone marrow—tissue that is also present in the bones of female birds to protect them from losing too much calcium when they lay eggs. So we know that B. rex was a girl, but we'll have to wait to know the sex of Black Beauty or, for that matter, whether Chicago's Field Museum may be in possession of the original "Boy Named Sue."

The Black Beauty—not the biggest, nor the most complete, but a Tyrannosaurus rex that every Albertan can take great pride in nonetheless.

Mammoths and Mastodons

AH, THE ELEPHANTS OF ANCIENT ALBERTA! Don't you just wish
there were still mammoths and mastodons roaming the province today?
They were here until quite recently in geological terms—right up until the
end of the Ice Age, some 10,000 years ago or so. Mammoths, or "wooly
mammoths," were the larger of the two sorts of extinct elephants and
they were indeed quite hairy compared to their living relatives. A big male
mammoth could weigh about four and a half to five tonnes, which is about
the weight of a big African elephant today. It is only a bit less than the esti-
mated weight of some familiar large dinosaurs such as *Tyrannosaurus* and
Triceratops. Mammoths had huge, sweeping tusks that they probably used
for defence from predators, for impressing one another and for sweeping
the snow off of plants in winter so they could feed their huge bodies.
Mastodons were about the same size as mammoths, perhaps a bit smaller
depending on the species, and they were still clearly elephant-like. They
had straighter tusks and smaller, bumpier teeth (for eating softer vegetation). Among both mammoths and mastodons, northern animals seem
to have been quite hairy, while those in the warm south were more like
modern elephants. In Alberta, the bones, teeth and tusks of mammoths
and mastodons are found not in the badlands, but in ancient river gravels.
The big rivers that traverse the province today did not take the same course
before the Ice Age, and there are places where the new river valley crosses
the old river valley, exposing the old gravels. Palaeontologists who study
Ice Age mammals also search in gravel pits, hoping they will find the fossils
before the gravel crusher does. And yes, we have a good fossil record of
these animals from Alberta, but no frozen mammoths yet—that's something unique to Siberia and Alaska so far.

The Wooly Mammoth skeleton at the Royal Tyrrell Museum, forever safeguarded from the imminent skeletal attack of a sabre-toothed cat. In life, which do you think would have triumphed?

The Milk River badlands, created from a different sort of rock than those farther north, also have a different look to them.

The Milk River

THE MILK RIVER is the southernmost river in Alberta, flowing into the Missouri River in Montana, and from there down into the Mississippi and ultimately to the Gulf of Mexico. Today, we find it surprising that water from Alberta flows all the way to the Gulf of Mexico—our only drainage basin that doesn't wind up in Hudson's Bay or the Arctic Ocean. An entire geological formation has been named the Milk River Formation, and it dates from about 80–84 million years ago, which makes it older than our other badlands by about five or more million years. The Milk River Formation is not as rich in terms of dinosaurs and other fossils, but it has produced some surprises. Approximately 13 different types of dinosaur fossils are known from the formation. They are generally found as fragmentary bones and as teeth, which makes them difficult to identify. In palaeontological circles, however, the Milk River Formation is probably best known for its mammal tooth fossils, found at a locality east of the town of Milk River. Some of these mammals appear later in the fossil record here than anywhere else we know of on Earth. For many Albertans, Writing-on-Stone Provincial Park is, of course, the best-known spot along the Milk River, but the Milk River Formation's greatest gift is the thick, relatively soft sandstone on which early aboriginal people carved petroglyph rock art. Protecting the petroglyphs from erosion is a lot harder than protecting fossils, since fossils can simply be removed and taken to the lab, so if you haven't seen the rock art of Writing-on-Stone Provincial Park, be sure to do so in the next decade or two, or it may be too late.

Mosasaurs, The Giant Marine Lizards

MOSASAURS WERE GIGANTIC SEA-GOING LIZARDS that lived in oceans around the world during the last part of the Age of Reptiles, the Late Cretaceous. They were true lizards, not dinosaurs, and in fact they included the largest lizards that ever lived. Some mosasaurs were as big as *Tyrannosaurus rex*, some 14 metres long, while the largest land lizards ever were five-metre monitors from Australia. The monitors, or goannas, have long been considered to be the closest relatives of mosasaurs, but recent work suggests this may not be the case after all. Among the lizards and snakes, the mosasaurs were by far the most highly aquatic of the lot, with flipper-like feet and long swimming tails. They are better adapted for the sea than the living sea snakes and Galapagos marine iguanas, and even the sea turtles. For one thing, they gave birth to live young at sea. They ate fish, other mosasaurs, and even the coil-shelled ammonite molluscs of the day, although work by Mount Royal College's Dr. Paul Johnston, who is also a reseach associate of the Royal Tyrrell Museum, has shown that the famous "tooth marks" of mosasaurs on ammonite shells are more likely to have been caused by snail-like molluscs. The jaws of mosasaurs could open super-wide, like those of a snake, and they could swallow large prey. Some had a bony extension at the front of the jaws, but it is not clear if they used this to ram other animals or not. Mosasaurs lived at a time when sea level was at an all-time high and there was a lot more near-shore shallow water than ever before or since. Some mosasaurs swam up coastal rivers as well. The mosasaurs lived after the dolphin-like (but still reptilian) ichthyosaurs, but alongside plesiosaurs. The last remaining mosasaurs and plesiosaurs became extinct along with the last dinosaurs. Mosasaurs were named for the Meuse River in the Netherlands—its Latin name, Mosa, means "the crossing." And of course, "saurus" means lizard. In Alberta, we have such mosasaurs as *Mosasaurus*, *Plioplatecarpus*, *Prognathodon* and something that is probably *Tylosaurus*. Mosasaur fossils are most common in the Bearpaw Formation of southern Alberta and all of our mosasaurs are also known from Saskatchewan. At the University of Alberta, Dr. Michael Caldwell is a mosasaur specialist, and we can be sure that new and intriguing details of mosasaur palaeontology will emerge over the next few years.

A Clidastes *mosasaur skeleton at the Royal Tyrrell Museum clearly showing the paddle-like feet that characterized the largest true lizards ever to live on Earth.*

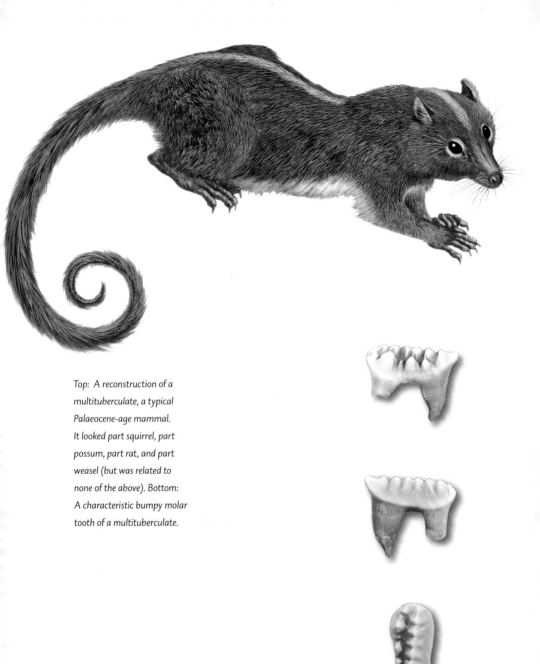

Top: A reconstruction of a
multituberculate, a typical
Palaeocene-age mammal.
It looked part squirrel, part
possum, part rat, and part
weasel (but was related to
none of the above). Bottom:
A characteristic bumpy molar
tooth of a multituberculate.

Multituberculates, Common but Extinct Mammals

MULTITUBERCULATES WERE MAMMALS. Ancient mammals. They first appeared during the time of the dinosaurs and they survived in good numbers well into the Age of Mammals, some 50 million years ago during the Eocene Epoch. To see an artist's reconstruction of your average multituberculate, you'd think it was some kind of squirrel, but its bones and teeth tell a different story. The teeth are downright peculiar. Up front, the incisors are long and thin, sort of like those of a rodent or a rabbit, but blunter. Then there is a gap, without teeth, followed by a huge slicing tooth on the lower jaw that sheared against a more rectangular cutting-board tooth on the upper jaw. The lower tooth looks like half of the blade from a table saw. Behind this shearing pair of teeth, the molars are rectangular, with rows of parallel bumps for grinding. As for the rest of the animal, we know it isn't related to living marsupials or the placental mammals we see in Alberta today, so it may be that multituberculates laid eggs and were otherwise quite unlike the mammals we are most familiar with now. In Alberta, fossils of multituberculates are common in the right kinds of rocks—those dating from the Late Cretaceous (the last part of the Age of Reptiles) right on into the Palaeocene Epoch. Rocks of this kind can be found near Calgary and Red Deer. Some palaeontologists have suggested that the multituberculates died out some time after the first rodents appeared, that is, well into the Age of Mammals, but others are not so sure. Just because multituberculates looked a bit like rodents doesn't mean that they were outcompeted by rodents—nature is rarely that simple. To me, it is much more interesting to note that the peculiar tooth arrangement of multituberculates evolved numerous times among mammals, not just once in the multituberculates. Some early primates had this sort of dentition, as do some living and extinct marsupials, including some sorts of possums and very small kangaroos called jerboa kangaroos or bettongs. So, the oddball teeth of multituberculates were not just some sort of primitive experiment that was inferior to the simpler teeth of rodents. Instead, the multituberculates were ahead of their time and numerous other lineages of mammals have evolved to be more multituberculate-like ever since.

Myledaphus, A Guitar Fish

MYLEDAPHUS BIPARTITUS WAS AN ANCIENT RAY— in the same group of fishes as living stingrays, manta rays and skates. *Myledaphus* is also a very common fossil in the badlands of Alberta, and is found in Late Cretaceous rocks dating back 65 to 80 million years before the present. For many years, however, all we knew about *Myledaphus* was its teeth. The teeth of *Myledaphus* are easy to recognize. They are small (half the size of a pea), although some grow to be pea-sized and have a peg-like shape. On the top, they are flat and six-sided, while the root is short and divided in two (hence the name *Myledaphus bipartitus*—"bipartite" means divided in two). The six-sided shape of the teeth is a clear indication that they were arranged in honeycomb fashion to produce a broad, flat crushing plate (the complete jaws in the new specimen show this to be true and there is a partial jaw found a few years ago that had already shown this). The fact that some living rays have teeth like this to crush clams and other hard-shelled invertebrates is good evidence to suggest that *Myledaphus* did too. In 1998, palaeontologists from the Royal Tyrrell Museum uncovered the first really great specimen of *Myledaphus* in the badlands of Dinosaur Provincial Park. Amazingly, the cartilage skeleton of this ray was heavily calcified and had been preserved along with the jaws containing the teeth and thousands of tiny hard denticles that once protected its skin. Usually, all of these structures either decay or simply wash away before the scattered teeth are fossilized. For the first time, we could see the outline of this fish, which actually looks a lot like palaeontologists thought it would! Originally, *Myledaphus* was thought to be a ray, but some later authors referred it to the group that contains the chimaera or "rat fish"—a group of fishes related to sharks and rays, and still common in the seas today. More recently, some have suggested it is a stingray with a venomous sting in its tail, just like living stingrays; however, this has always been a problem as no "stingers" were ever found even where teeth are common. And now that we have the actual skeleton, what is the answer? It's a guitarfish! (This has been suspected at least since the late 1980s). So, what's a guitarfish, you ask? It's a type of ray with living relatives, some of which have long snouts and look a very tiny bit like a guitar. Most fossil guitarfish, on the other hand, had short snouts and look more like stingrays without stings.

The finest *Myledaphus* fossil ever found (from Dinosaur Provincial Park), showing about half of the body, minus the tail. Inset: The crushing, six-sided teeth of this ancient guitarfish.

New Fossil Names

PALAEONTOLOGISTS ARE OFTEN ASKED, "Have you ever discovered a new kind of extinct creature? Did you get to name it after yourself?" Well, despite how common this question is, the real situation is quite different. For one thing, it is bad form to name a species in your own honour, and no one does it. On the other hand, every time a palaeontologist names a new species, that palaeontologist's name appears at the end of the species name, along with the year that the name was first published. For example, the full name of *Tyrannosaurus rex* is really *Tyrannosaurus rex* Osborn 1905. Henry Fairfield Osborn is the so-called "author" of the species name. Few people other than working taxonomists use these full versions of scientific names, but they do exist and they are important for establishing the exact origins and histories of names. As for naming a species new to science after someone else, that is up to the author, who is free to name the species after a person, a place, a characteristic of the fossil, or even a "random combination of letters." For example, Rodolfo Coria, a palaeontologist in Argentina, named the meat-eating dinosaur *Quilmesaurus curriei* to honour Dr. Philip Currie of Albertan fame. Names honouring men end in -i, those honouring women end in -ae, such as *Ptilodus kummae*, named for Linda Kumm, now Linda Strong-Watson, a former technician at the University of Alberta and the Royal Tyrrell Museum. Names honouring groups of people end in -orum, such as *Bambiraptor feinbergorum*, named by Philip Currie and five of his colleagues as a note of thanks to a family named Feinberg. It is always a pleasure to have something named for you, but it is by no means the reason palaeontologists look for new things. And yes, I am happy to report that in the Northwest Territories there is a trilobite species known from 450 million-year old Ordovician rocks that bears the name *Cybeloides acorni*, named by palaeontologist Brenda Hunda to thank me for encouraging her career way back when she was still in high school and early university.

"Tyrannosaurus rex Osborn 1905," featuring the Huxley, Alberta skeleton (on display at the Royal Tyrrell Museum) and the original drawing by E.S. Christman taken from Osborn's description of the species.

The Oil Sands

EVERY ALBERTAN HAS HEARD OF THE OIL SANDS (or the tar sands, as they are called), but how many of us consider them part of our deep geological heritage? And how many people know how they came to be? I got the story from Dr. Murray Gingras at the University of Alberta, and to hear him tell it, this was a tale of great scientific detective work. It turns out that in the Early Cretaceous Period, with the mountains beginning to rise up in the west and the sea beginning to flood the northern part of the province, there were three main valleys draining the province to the north. One of these— the easternmost valley—was the McMurray Channel, and where it met the sea, it deposited huge amounts of sand. This has been known for some time. Now to geologists, the real breakthrough in their understanding of all this sand came in the 1980s with the work of Dr. George Pemberton, also of the University of Alberta. He showed that the area was under the influence of tides. As a result, some people envision something like Chesapeake Bay, a huge tidal estuary, while others see it more like a tidal river delta. Either way, the sand (all 2.5 trillion cubic metres of it) came in both by the actions of the river and the actions of the tides. The work of another geologist, Mike Ranger, has suggested the sand deposit was trapped under other sediments in what is called a "rollover anticline" (a term I quite like, because it means that the sediments formed a sort of giant inverted bowl after the lower layers dissolved away), and this anticline is what trapped the oil that came from much older rocks and moved up into the sand. Then the oil was changed to bitumen by the actions of bacteria and percolating rainwater—it became thicker and heavier, and was then more or less solidified in place, making oil sand petroleum extraction the pain in the butt that it is today. And what does this have to do with fossils? Well, for one thing, the burrows of filter-feeding worms called *Cylindrichnus* were pivotal in scientifically establishing the tidal nature of the environment. And in the sediments just above the McMurray Formation oil sands, there are also wonderful skeletons of marine reptiles (ichthyosaurs and plesiosaurs) that moved in when the sea finally overtook and flooded the land. So there you have it—an economic boon, a geological wonder and a fossil bed to be proud of: the Fort McMurray Oil Sands.

*The tar sands and the machines
that process it—an Alberta
marvel created by dinosaur-
aged sand trapping much older
oil and changing it to bitumen
over vast periods of time.*

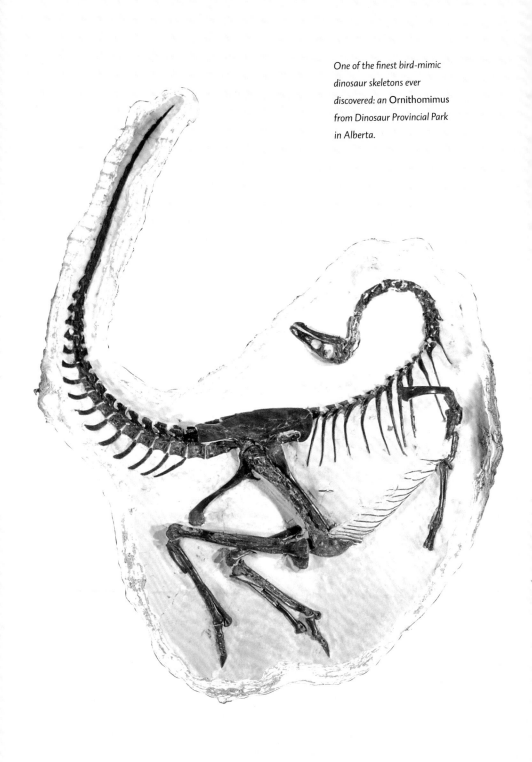

One of the finest bird-mimic dinosaur skeletons ever discovered: an Ornithomimus from Dinosaur Provincial Park in Alberta.

Ornithomimids, The Bird Mimics

BIRD MIMIC DINOSAURS—the name sounds terribly modern, since
the bird-dinosaur connection seems to be the hottest theme in palaeontology these days. But the so-called bird mimic dinosaurs in the family
Ornithomimidae (which means "bird mimic") have been known since 1890
when the first bird mimic, *Ornithomimus* itself, was described by Othniel
Marsh based on fossils from the western United States. The name "bird
mimic" was an unfortunate choice. In biology, when one animal mimics
another, the resemblance is intended to protect the mimic. For example,
non-venomous red, yellow and black-banded snakes mimic dangerous
coral snakes, and as a result predators avoid eating both, since they are
not as observant as biologists when it comes to telling the two apart. But
the bird mimic dinosaurs did not "mimic" birds. Ornithomimids were
around during the Cretaceous Period, and they were people-sized or
bigger and ran on two legs. They had grasping hands instead of wings
and they had a long tail supported by vertebrae, not a feathery tail like
a bird. Their jaws were, however, toothless, and supported a beak like
that of a bird. In other words, they were bird-like, but they were not bird
mimics. Our two Albertan types were *Ornithomimus* and *Struthiomimus*
(*Struthiomimus* meaning "ostrich mimic"). So why, if these dinosaurs
were so terribly and obviously bird-like, did it take so long for palaeontologists to come up with the hypothesis that birds came from a dinosaur
ancestor? Quite frankly, I think that's a very good question. In defence of
the early palaeontologists, however, it has long been clear that the orntho-
mimids themselves were too big and lived too late in the game to be the
ancestors of such things as *Archaeopteryx*, the earliest known bird-dinosaur intermediate, which lived during the Jurassic Period, the geological
period before the Cretaceous. But the birdishness of the ornithomimids
did indeed start some foreheads wrinkling, even back in the late 1800s—
and it took more than 100 years for the idea to gain favour. Of course, if
there's one thing tougher than reconstructing prehistory from fossils,
it's reconstructing the way someone's thought processes worked long
before you were born. The connection between bird-mimic dinosaurs and
birds was ignored, the same way the connection between other primates
and human beings was ignored before the writings of Charles Darwin.

Pachyrhinosaurus, The Thick-nosed Dinosaur

PACHYRHINOSAURUS means "thick-nosed lizard." Long before the Royal Tyrrell Museum opened its doors, the first-ever discovered skull of a *Pachyrhinosaurus* was the star attraction at the Drumheller Town Museum. Visitors would marvel at the skull, which looked much like that of *Triceratops*, but without the long pointy horns. Instead, it had what looked like a broken-off tree trunk on the top of its snout, leading some of us to call it "Old Stump Face." *Pachyrhinosaurus* was often reconstructed as a battering-ram dinosaur that used its stump-like nasal horn to batter its enemies, or more likely its competitors, within the *Pachyrhinosaurus* clan. It was about six metres long and probably weighed about a tonne and a half, fully grown. Palaeontologist Charlie Sternberg named this dinosaur *Pachyrhinosaurus canadensis* in 1950, and for a long time all that we knew of it was this single skull in the Drumheller Museum. Then more bones turned up. Surprisingly, however, they were not from the Drumheller area—they were from up north, in Alaska and near Grande Prairie in the now-famous Pipestone Creek bonebed. These northern *Pachyrhinosaurus* fossils cleared up some of the mystery surrounding this dinosaur, but they also inspired new questions. Some see the broad geographic range of this animal, from Alaska to southern Alberta, as evidence that this dinosaur migrated north and south with the seasons. But others point out that animals such as moose have the same distribution today and don't migrate at all. It may be that the northern and southern specimens are not even from the same species. Some see the bonebed, containing more than 2,000 jumbled bones, as evidence that a herd died in a flood while travelling together. Others cautiously argue that jumbled bones tell you nothing about how the animals died, but only about how rivers pile bones together in the same way they also create log-jams. Logs don't travel in herds, so why should jumbled bones? Clearly, *Pachyrhinosaurus* still has some secrets to unveil and it is fortunate that enthusiasm for palaeontology is growing in the Grande Prairie area. Perhaps soon we will have a better understanding of this spectacular Alberta dinosaur.

A composite skeleton of **Pachyrhinosaurus** created from isolated bones from near Grande Prairie—
still an enigmatic dinosaur that is only slowly giving up its secrets.

A palaeontology technician at work "preparing" a fossil at the Royal Tyrrell Museum. Not all palaeontological careers involve being a professor or museum curator.

Palaeontology in Alberta

PALAEONTOLOGISTS ARE SOME OF THE HIGHEST PROFILE scientists
in Alberta, but how many people are there in the palaeontology biz
anyway? And while it's nice to think that the Royal Tyrrell Museum
is the hub of the palaeo wheel in our province, the truth is, of course,
more complicated. At the Museum, there are curators, technicians and
administrators. Most of these people were trained at universities and sure
enough there are professors of palaeontology at both the University of
Alberta in Edmonton and the University of Calgary. These institutions also
hire technicians and other support staff. Then there are the government
palaeontologists in places like the Geological Survey of Canada. The oil
industry also enlists the help of palaeontologists. Finding oil requires a
detailed understanding of the complex three-dimensional underground
map that petroleum geologists have developed for Alberta. That means
interpreting drill cores, and one of the best ways to determine the age
of rocks in a drill core is to identify and analyze such things as fossil
microplankton and the tiny fossils called conodonts, the jaws of ancient
parasitic creatures related to lampreys and fishes. In fact, it's not an
exaggeration to say that the Alberta economy, at least the petroleum-
driven part of the Alberta economy, is directly dependent on the science of
palaeontology (despite a strong media bias toward the more spectacular
fossils from the dinosaur age). And some people also make their living
by catering to the public's interest in fossils. Palaeontology tourism is a
big part of our province's economy and there are also broadcasters and
writers (such as myself), sculptors and artists, and even entire companies,
that cast and mount dinosaur skeletons and other fossils for museums
around the world. There may only be one or two people paid to do full-time
research on dinosaurs in the province, but the world of palaeontology is
much bigger than that. And if you happen to be a young person planning
a palaeontology career, my advice is to stay focused but remain flexible.
There are plenty of ways to make palaeontology your life's work.

Pantodonts, Giant Palaeocene Mammals

AT THE END OF THE AGE OF DINOSAURS, mammals took over and have ruled the Earth ever since...right? Well, sort of. The truth is that mammals were around since the first dinosaurs appeared, and for at least 10 million years after the last of the dinosaurs, most mammals remained quite small. Even today, the average size of a mammal is somewhere in the squirrel range, if not smaller. The period following the end-Cretaceous extinction is called the Palaeocene Epoch, and I am always amazed by the fascinating world of small mammals that has come to light through the discovery of teeth and partial skeletons around Red Deer, mainly by Dr. Richard Fox of the University of Alberta and his students. But what about the biggest and most impressive Palaeocene mammals of all, the pantodonts? From the valley of the Red Deer River, west of Red Deer itself, we now have two very fine specimens of pantodonts, in the genus *Titanoides*, plus many isolated bits and pieces. To my eye, they look something like a cross between a wolf, a bear and a ground sloth, with big canine teeth and strong bones and claws. Most palaeontologists agree that they were probably herbivores or omnivores, especially since later pantodonts (from other places) were more obviously herbivorous. But the main thing that is impressive about pant-odonts is their size—they are about the size of a small cow and no other mammals from that time come close. When I look at the skull of *Titanoides* (and there is one on display at the Royal Tyrrell Museum), I see a fear-some-looking animal. But clearly the molar and premolar teeth were those of a plant eater. And the claws were the claws of a digger, not a meat eater. But those big canine teeth? Well, some think they were for digging as well, while others interpret them as display teeth, intended to impress other *Titanoides*. It just doesn't seem right that the giant of the Palaeocene was a predator while all of its prey remained tiny and squirrel-like, but this is probably one of those cases where the only real test would be a trip through the time machine, something we at the Royal Tyrrell Museum have been wanting to do for some time now as well.

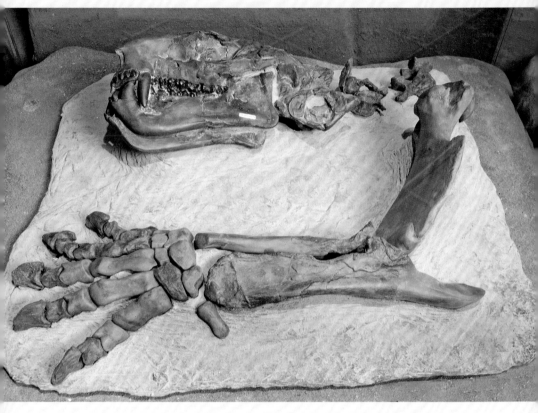

The skull and forelimb of Titanoides look fearsome, but try to imagine this Palaeocene-aged giant mammal as a peaceful, digging plant eater.

The long-skulled, duck-billed Parasaurolophus, one of the classic dinosaurs that all kids recognize, was originally discovered right here in Alberta.

Parasaurolophus, A Long-headed Duck-bill

PARA-sauro-LO-phus. Or perhaps you pronounce it PARA-saur-AWL-ophus? I have heard it both ways, and since there is no truly official way to pronounce dinosaur names, either way works for me. *Parasaurolophus* is one of the most famous duck-billed dinosaurs—you know, the one with the long tubular crest sweeping back over its neck from the top of its head. Some reconstructions show this dinosaur with a flag-like flap of skin between the crest and the head, but we have no real evidence for such a thing. The crest probably just stuck out behind the head like a backward-facing horn. Still, the crest is, or was, impressive. Some palaeontologists have suggested that there were long-crested and short-crested *Parasaurolophus* and that the short-crested forms were probably the females. It seems likely that the crests were used both for sound production (because they were hollow and connected to the breathing passage) and to allow other *Parasaurolophus* to recognize members of their own species. After all, other sorts of duck-billed dinosaurs had differently-shaped crests, or no crests at all. Unfortunately for all of us, *Parasaurolophus* fossils are actually quite rare. This dinosaur is known from Dinosaur Provincial Park and a few other places here and there—even as far away as New Mexico. It seems that there were probably three species of *Parasaurolophus*, each slightly different from the others. And what does such a cumbersome name mean? *Para* means near, *sauro* means lizard, and *lophus* means crested. All this information only makes sense if you already know that there is another sort of duck-billed dinosaur named *Saurolophus*. So *Parasaurolophus* is "near" *Saurolophus*. And you deep dino-geeks out there will also know of *Prosaurolophus*, whose name means "before" *Saurolophus*. It all makes perfect sense, even though it's really not very interesting when you get right down to it. But the dinosaurs themselves are tremendously interesting no matter what you call them!

Parksosaurus, Park's Dinosaur

PARKSOSAURUS was a smallish dinosaur, only about two-and-a-half metres long. It had no horns or other weird anatomical attributes, and it ate plants. So, it's not exactly on the tip of every six-year-old kid's tongue when it comes to favourite dinosaur names. *Parksosaurus* was discovered near Drumheller and is known only from partial remains. It walked on its hind legs and was distantly related to the much larger duck-billed dinosaurs. In its day, if there had been palaeontologists around to think about it, they would probably have considered *Parksosaurus* to be a kind of living fossil, since it was much like the ancestor of the duck-bills, a creature that undoubtedly lived much earlier in the Age of Reptiles. Charles M. Sternberg named *Parksosaurus* in 1937 to honour William Parks, a Canadian palaeontologist. Ironically, Parks himself wrote the first description of *Parksosaurus*, but he gave it the wrong name by considering it a member of the genus *Thescelosaurus*. Parks intended to honour a woman whose last name was Warren, and called his dinosaur *Thescelosaurus warreni*. When it was later determined that Sternberg's genus name was the correct one, the new combination became *Parksosaurus warreni*, honouring both Parks and Warren, something that must have pleased William Parks. But the name was changed again, from *warreni* (which refers to a man) to *warrenae* (which refers to a woman). So the final product is *Parksosaurus warrenae*, although some palaeontologists are now considering putting the dinosaur back in the genus *Thescelosaurus*. And you thought palaeontology was all about adventure and being outside with a pick and shovel. *Parksosaurus*, in many books, is placed in a group called the Hypsilophodontidae and the general idea has long been that the hypsilophodontids gave rise to the iguanodontids (you know, the European dinosaurs with big thumb spikes) and the iguanodontids gave rise to the duck-billed dinosaurs. Not everyone agrees on this, but picture one family tree growing out of another family tree growing out of yet another family tree, but with skinny little branches of the first tree growing right up beside the top of the third tree. One of those skinny branches represents *Parksosaurus*—one of Alberta's most obscure dinosaurs to be sure, but still an interesting part of our palaeontological heritage.

Top: A jovial-looking William Parks (on the right), with, from left to right, Levi Sternberg, Loris Russell and an unidentified third companion. Bottom: The dinosaur that honours William Parks, Parkosaurus warrenae.

The World's Oldest Pike

ESOX TIEMANI lived near the Smoky River in Alberta some 50 million years ago. It was discovered in the early 1980s by Burt Tieman of Grand Prairie, who was working on oil and gas access roads when he spotted the outline of a fish on a piece of shale. The specimen made its way to the University of Alberta, where, for a time, it sat on a lab bench awaiting attention from the scientists. From the location, they knew it was Palaeocene in age, from the period after the extinction of the dinosaurs, but no one had yet figured out what it really was. Then, according to legend, an entomologist (of all people) stopped by the lab and remarked, "Hey, that looks like a pike—is that what it is?" And yes, he was right. Dr. Mark Wilson formally described the specimen in 1984 and named it *Esox tiemani* in honour of Mr. Tieman, the man who discovered the specimen. If you want to see *Esox tiemani*, it is now in the Grand Prairie Museum, or you can see a cast of it on display at the Royal Tyrrell Museum. At the time of its discovery, it was considered the world's oldest pike, but now we know that there were pike around during the time of the dinosaurs, in the Cretaceous Period. These

The type specimen of Esox tiemani, *the world's oldest pike, looks a lot like the northern pike that live in Alberta today.*

fossils, mostly of jaws and backbones, are also known from Alberta, so Alberta still holds the record for the world's oldest pike. The world's oldest member of the trout family, on the other hand, was discovered in British Columbia. Its name is *Eosalmo driftwoodensis,* but it too was described by Mark Wilson, an Albertan. Anglers will be pleased to know that pike haven't changed much over the last 70 million years except that they are much bigger. *Esox tiemani* was a fair-sized fish—the original fossil is of a year-old fish almost half a metre long. *Esox lucius,* on the other hand, is the northern pike we all know and love, and there are other *Esox* living today as well, but not in Alberta—things such as chain pickerel, grass pickerel and muskellunge or "muskies." And do remember that we have numerous English names in Alberta for the northern pike, such as jack, jackfish, slough shark and (for small ones) "hammer handles." In a way, I find it satisfying that a "living fossil" has made such a deep connection with Alberta culture today.

Plants of the Ornithomimid Quarry

PALAEONTOLOGISTS ARE COURTEOUS, co-operative people...up to a point. That's why it was such a difficult job to get all the fossils out without damage when the finest skeleton of a bird-mimic ornithomimid dinosaur ever found in Alberta was revealed just underneath a bed of very nicely preserved fossil plants. At a recent conference, the dinosaur scientists told jokes about the plants "contaminating" the quarry and slowing down their work, while the palaeobotanists joked about the tragedy of having "struck dinosaur" during a perfectly good search for fossil plants. The truth is, we more or less knew what the dinosaur was going to look like (although it is a truly beautiful skeleton), but the plants were a great surprise. The site in question is in Dinosaur Provincial Park, and therefore dates back to about 75 million years ago, a time when the record of fossil plants in Alberta is remarkably slim. So it was a real thrill for Dr. Ruth Stockey of the University of Alberta to have the chance to study this rare window on the vegetation of Cretaceous Alberta. One interesting plant was a well-preserved floating water plant that belonged in a group called the aroids, or the order Arales—a group that also included climbing vines, as well as the living duckweeds and water lettuce or *Pistia*. The fossil floating plant, tentatively called *Pistia corrugata*, is apparently not a real *Pistia* and will soon be given its own name. This is evidence that floating plants evolved not once but three times in the order Arales, which, in botanical terms, is nifty news. Another Dinosaur Park discovery was particularly striking. There, in the rock, lay what any one of us would immediately identify as a ginger root, much like any ginger root you could buy in a grocery store today. The palaeontologists are quick to say that it was not ginger *per se*, but rather a member of the ginger family, but it's clear that something very much like ginger was growing underfoot back then. Once the dinosaur times were over, the record of fossil plants in Alberta improves, and there are many good sites for fossil leaves in the Red Deer area and elsewhere. But for now, some of the best fossil plants from the Late Cretaceous come to us from around the body of a long-dead bird-mimic dinosaur.

The famous ornithomimid quarry—famous as much for the plants that lay overtop the dinosaur, as for the dinosaur itself.

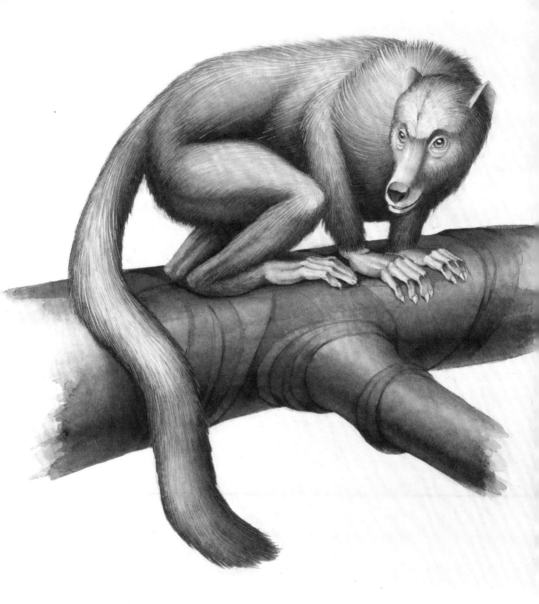

Plesiadapis was an odd early primate, although most of its oddities lay in its teeth. Here, it looks a bit squirrelish, a bit wolfish, and hauntingly humanoid in the shape of its hands.

Plesiadapis, A Weird Early Primate

PLESIADAPIS WAS A PRIMATE, but a very ancient primate that was quite unlike any lemur, tarsier, monkey or ape living today. The most so-called primitive living primates are called tree shrews, and they are vaguely squirrel-like creatures, recognizable as primates only by their teeth and the details of their anatomy. Likewise, *Plesiadapis* and its relatives were also squirrel-like and not at all like the bigger-brained primates that would follow later in Earth history. No, *Plesiadapis* was on a side-branch of the primate family tree, but a side branch that was quite successful during the Palaeocene Epoch, the time period that followed the extinction of the dino-saurs. Among the general public, Alberta is best known for its Cretaceous fossils—the dinosaurs and their contemporaries. But among palaeon-tologists it is equally famous for the Palaeocene fossils that have been discovered in central Alberta (around Red Deer) and in the southern foot-hills. There, a number of species of *Plesiadapis* have been uncovered and their fossils correlated with relatives from throughout the western US east of the Rocky Mountains. Some palaeontologists have even suggested using the sequence of *Plesiadapis* to identify "*Plesiadapis* zones" in order to date the rocks in which their fossil teeth are found. In one locality in Wyoming, *Plesiadapis* became famous as part of a debate about the tempo of evolution. Stephen J. Gould of Harvard and Niles Eldridge of the American Museum of Natural History had famously suggested that evolu-tion proceeds in quick jumps, separated by long periods of little or no change, by what they called "punctuated equilibrium." But Philip Gingerich from the University of Michigan used the fossils of a series of species of *Plesiadapis* and its primate relatives that had been taken from beds in which fossils were continuously being deposited over millions of years to show that at least these mammals had changed gradually, the way Darwin orig-inally envisioned (and which we now call "gradualism"). And what does *Plesiadapis* mean? Well, *Adapis* is another fossil primate that lived much later than *Plesiadapis*. And "plesio" means "near," although we now realize they were distantly related and not "near" in any important sense of the word.

Plesiosaurs, The Sea Serpents of the Mesozoic

PLESIOSAURS WERE MARINE REPTILES that lived at the same time as the dinosaurs. Their name, oddly enough, means "near lizards," but they were neither lizards nor dinosaurs, and they are certainly not near lizards in any normal sense of the phrase. The best-known plesiosaurs were long-necked "Loch Ness Monster"-type creatures, but the group also included animals with shorter necks. All had flipper-like legs that served as underwater wings for "flying" through the water and all were fully aquatic. They probably ate fish. In Alberta, there are a number of plesiosaur fossils known from the badlands, especially in what we call the Bearpaw Formation of rock. These rocks were laid down in salt water in the interior seaway we call the Bearpaw Sea. Bearpaw sediments generally do not contain the remains of dinosaurs, but they do preserve such things as plesiosaurs, mosasaurs and other marine reptiles. This is not to say, however, that all plesiosaurs lived in the sea. In places like Dinosaur Provincial Park, where the rocks were laid down in rivers and shallow estuaries, we do find the occasional plesiosaur fossils as well. Perhaps these were sea-going plesiosaurs that swam up the rivers, or perhaps they were a separate sort of plesiosaur altogether. Of course, I know what most of you are wondering—does a living plesiosaur survive today in Loch Ness, in Scotland? In my opinion... no! In fact there is a very fine book on the subject, published in 1984 and written by Ronald Binns, that convincingly traces the story of the Loch Ness Monster to a few innocent sightings of otters and ducks and the zeal of an imaginative newspaper reporter. Some of you, however, will remember Alberta's own supposed plesiosaur, the Heart Lake Monster of the 1980s. Zoologists I spoke to from the University of Alberta who investigated the monster at the time came back pretty much convinced it was a moose. And in 1983 the *Edmonton Journal* published a photograph of the skull of the Heart Lake Monster. Many of us wrote in to say we recognized the skull... as that of a deer—a White-tailed Deer as I recall. Sigh. A plesiosaur would have been so much more exciting, but for the moment we will all have to make peace with the disappointing fact that the last truly conclusive record of a plesiosaur anywhere on Earth comes from about 65 million years ago.

The skeleton of a short-necked plesiosaur, or pliosaur, on display at the Royal Tyrrell Museum.

"Primitive" Plants

DO YOU EVER LOOK IN THE BACKGROUND of dinosaur paintings? There you will see the under-appreciated work of palaeobotanists, the people who study fossil plants. There are also people who study fossil pollen, called palynologists, such as Dennis Braman at the Royal Tyrrell Museum, whose work greatly increases our understanding of ancient flora. But here I want to talk about fossil leaves, stems, roots and wood—in other words, fossil plants that we can easily identify. As you may know, petrified wood is the provincial stone of Alberta and most of our petrified wood comes from the Late Cretaceous, when the dinosaurs of Drumheller and Dinosaur Provincial Park were around. Yes, there were trees back then and most of the trees were conifers. Eva Koppelhus, a palaeobotanist and wife of the famous dinosaur man Phil Currie, has recently undertaken a study of this fossil wood. Conifers are considered primitive plants and another even more primitive plant that was reasonably common in the Late Cretaceous was the horsetail. Today, we find horsetails quite commonly as small plants, rarely higher than your knee. Their stems are jointed about every two to three centimetres and they reproduce by spores. I'm sure you have seen them. The pioneers called them "scouring rush" since you could crush them and use their silica-rich stems to clean out pots and such, sort of. Before the Age of the Dinosaurs there were tree-sized horsetails, but by the end of the Cretaceous Period they were much like those we see today. Cycads were also present in the dinosaur times, and most Albertans have only seen cycads in greenhouses and conservatories. They generally grow as a whorl of heavy leaves surrounding a central cone-like structure. Cycads haven't changed much since the Cretaceous Period, and neither have some conifers and horsetails. Palaeobotanists are quick to point out that these so-called living fossils are often over-represented in palaeontological art, since it is easy to paint them from living models. In truth, they say, there were more sorts of odd flowering plants living in dinosaurian times than we generally let on, but we just don't know what they looked like, so we leave them out of our paintings and dioramas.

A fossilized tree stump surrounded by ferns and mosses, both of which are living representatives of so-called "primitive" plants and can be viewed in the Royal Tyrrell Museum's Cretaceous Garden.

Pterosaurs, The Flying Reptiles

PTEROSAURS WERE FLYING REPTILES—wonderful creatures—but they were not dinosaurs. The pterosaurs were the second group of flapping animals capable of self-powered flight to appear (insects were the first), and the first pterosaurs appeared about 30 million years before the first birds. Which means that pterosaurs arose alongside the earliest dinosaurs and died out alongside the last dinosaurs. In fact, they were part of the "archosaur" group that includes dinosaurs, birds, crocodilians and pterosaurs. The biggest pterosaurs were bigger than any bird, while the smallest were sparrow-sized. Like birds, they had hollow bones for lightness and flight. Many pterosaurs probably ate fish, and their fossils are almost exclusively found in marine sediments. The wings of pterosaurs were formed from a skin membrane that stretched from the extended fourth finger of the hand to the hind leg and often between the hind legs. The wing was stiff toward the tip, at least in some pterosaurs, and there is evidence that some were also covered with a hair-like coat for insulation. Much of our understanding here comes from the Russian pterosaur *Sordes pilosus* and new finds from Liaoning in China. There are very few pterosaur fossils from Alberta, and all are fragmentary, with only one partial skeleton known. Apparently we had at least two types, both of which were typical Cretaceous pterosaurs, not the long-tailed Jurassic variety. The first was an enormous creature, with a wingspan ranging from six to 11 metres, possibly a member of the famous genera *Quetzalcoatlus* or *Montanazhdarcho.* The second is an unknown smaller pterosaur, known only from partial finger bones. I was there when one of these fossils was found at Dinosaur Provincial Park in 1980. The fossil was only the size of a peanut and I have often thought how easy it would have been for that bone to wash downhill and into the river, or to disappear in someone's pocket. Every fossil, no matter how small, can be an important bit of evidence in the science of palaeontology and that is why fossils are so carefully protected here in Alberta.

Three gigantic Quetzalcoatlus soar in formation over the coastal plains of western Canada, creating a spectacle the likes of which the Earth has never seen since.

A mudpuppy salamander with frilly red gills on the sides of its head, possibly much like some of the salamanders that lived in Alberta during dinosaur times.

Fossil Salamanders

SALAMANDERS ARE REASONABLY FAMILIAR ANIMALS in Alberta
today, but we have only two species living in the province right now.
One, the Tiger Salamander, sometimes shows up in basements or in the
damp control boxes for lawn sprinkler systems. The other, the Long-toed
Salamander, is a rare creature that lives in mountain ponds. Salamanders
are amphibians and their young live in water, breathing with gills. Fossil
salamanders are also known from Alberta and there were certainly
salamanders here during the Cretaceous Period when the most famous
of the Alberta dinosaurs were roaming the deltas and lowlands of the
time. Usually, we find only their vertebrae—isolated backbones with a
distinctive shape and structure. But sometimes jaws or more complete
specimens turn up. One of the most commonly encountered groups of
fossil "salamanders" turns out not to be a salamander at all, but a closely
related group, the Albanerpetontidae. Today, there are more species of
salamanders in the eastern United States, and in particular the Appalachian
Mountains, than anywhere else on Earth. These are mostly lungless
salamanders that are able to breathe through their skin. The tremendous
diversity of these animals tells us two things. First, salamanders are still
evolving and diversifying. Second, salamanders were not, despite what
you might think, more successful in so-called primitive times, and they
are currently not more successful in the steamy tropics (unless, like many
Albertans, you consider the eastern US to be part of the steamy tropics).
The truth is that although salamanders, like frogs, are amphibians, they
are not necessarily ancient, nor primitive, amphibians. They appeared on
Earth well into the Age of Reptiles, some 150 million years ago, and they
continue to be important and interesting members of our animal fauna.

Sandy Point

EVER HEAR OF SANDY POINT, ALBERTA? I didn't think so. Yet this is one of the finest fossil sites in the province, right where Highway 41 crosses the South Saskatchewan River, about an hour's drive north of Medicine Hat. Over the years, the municipal campground at Sandy Point has been home to a great number of palaeontologists exploring the Cretaceous badlands for dinosaurs and other fossils. One prominent palaeontologist, David Krause, grew up on a ranch south of Sandy Point, where he was inspired by the fossil treasures around him. When I first visited Sandy Point, it was known as a bit of a party spot, so to speak, and was often a real mess, but in recent years the presence of a volunteer campground attendant and her husband has made it a very pleasant place to camp. And because it is the only access point on the South Saskatchewan between Medicine Hat and the Saskatchewan border, the Sandy Point campground is also important to canoeists and to naturalists like me who are interested in everything from birds to beetles. The badlands around Sandy Point are on private land, so don't plan a trip there and expect Dinosaur Provincial Park or Horseshoe Canyon. To look for fossils on private land, you need landowner permission and you need to abide by the rules for fossil hunting in Alberta, especially the rule that says "don't dig anything up without a permit." But amateur fossil hunters have made interesting discoveries at Sandy Point, as well as elsewhere in the province, so don't let me discourage you from looking, even alongside the road. The Sandy Point badlands, at least the layers that have produced fossils, are of equivalent age to those in Dinosaur Provincial Park, and have produced good specimens of a juvenile *Albertosaurus*, duck-billed dinosaurs, the armoured dinosaur *Euoplocephalus*, and a bonebed of *Centrosaurus* dinosaur bones. In other words, the same wonderworld of dinosaurs that we know from Dinosaur Provincial Park has also left evidence in the hills around Sandy Point.

The river valley near Sandy Point has produced some of the finest dinosaur fossils in Alberta, despite its low profile and humble facilities. Bottom: The lower jaw of Albertosaurus, from the rocks near Sandy Point.

The reconstructed skeleton of *Saurornitholestes, a lean, mean "raptor" about as big as a medium sized dog.*

Saurornitholestes, A Raptor

IF THERE ARE ANY CHILDREN READING THIS BOOK, here is my
challenge to you. We all know that it's impressive to hear kids spin off
names like *Tyrannosaurus*, *Stegosaurus* and *Parasaurolophus*, but these are
not the trickiest dinosaur names by far. How about the small Albertan
meat-eater *Saurornitholestes*? Can you say that *and* remember it? And
do you know how it is different from *Saurornithoides*, *Sinornithoides*,
Sinosauropteryx and *Sinornithosaurus*? Woof! That's the sort of thing
that separates the true palaeontology fanatics from the mere dabblers!
Saurornitholestes means "lizard-bird-stealer" and refers to the somewhat
bird-like, but still reptilian nature of the fossil, and its grasping claws
that may have been good for "stealing" so to speak. An amateur fossil
hunter, Mrs. Irene Vanderloh of Cessford, Alberta, discovered it in
Dinosaur Provincial Park. That was in 1974, and she brought her find to
the attention of Dr. John Storer, then of the Provincial Museum. Storer
was not a dinosaur specialist, so it fell to Hans-Dieter Sues to describe
and name the animal. Hans-Dieter was then a graduate student at the
University of Alberta and is now a scientist with the Carnegie Museum.
His description of *Saurornitholestes langstoni* appeared in 1978 and
the name also honours Wann Langston, a Texan palaeontologist who
worked here in Alberta, primarily in the 1950s. Now, in terms of its
relationships, *Saurornitholestes* was a dromaeosaurid, or a "raptor"
in modern terms. In fact, it appears to have been the most common
member of this family in its day. *Dromaeosaurus* is probably a more
famous dinosaur, but the isolated teeth of *Saurornitholestes* are much
more common than those of *Dromaeosaurus*, and the bones of both are
very rare. And how do you tell two meat-eating dinosaurs apart just by
their teeth? Well, on the teeth of *Saurornitholestes*, the cutting bumps or
denticles are much larger on the rear of the tooth than on the front. This
is not the case in *Dromaeosaurus*—one more example of how every little
detail helps flesh out our understanding of the Alberta Cretaceous.

Short-faced Bear

MOST PEOPLE HAVE HEARD OF THE CAVE BEAR—a gigantic extinct bear that lived alongside the cave men during the Ice Age and no doubt made life just a tad more terrifying than you and I can truly imagine. Cave bears and people no doubt competed for places to live and for food, not to mention probably hunted one another. Well, the good news is that there never were cave bears (*Ursus spelaeus*) in North America—they were a European phenomenon entirely, related to the brown and grizzly bears. Another sort of cave bear lived in the Ural Mountains of Asia and there was a sort of cave bear in Florida, but it was more like the South American spectacled bear and never came this far north. Here in Alberta, we had short-faced bears. In fact, the giant short-faced bear (*Arctodus simus*) was the biggest bear ever, period. It could reach more than four metres high without really trying. But don't just picture a huge grizzly with a short nose. Instead, the short-faced bear was lean and long-legged, and its short jaws were probably an adaptation to give it a more powerful bone-crushing bite. The short-faced bear was, like the Florida cave bear, more closely related to spectacled bears than to grizzlies or black bears, but that doesn't mean it was a dozy vegetarian like its living cousins. Instead, like other big extinct meat eaters, it has generated a debate about whether it was a predator or a scavenger. Personally, I would not be surprised if it were both. The last of the short-faced bears died out around the time the Ice Age ended about 10,000 years ago. This corresponds with four events, any one of which may have caused the extinction of these impressive animals (along with many other large mammals at the same time). First, people arrived and may have simply killed the bears with spears. Second, other sorts of bears, most notably grizzlies, also came to North America over the Bering land bridge between Alaska and Siberia, and they may have out-competed the short-faced bears. Third, the climate changed, and with it the vegetation and any number of potential bear-food items. And finally, some recent research at Berkeley has suggested that the shock wave from an exploding star—a supernova—hit the Earth at about this same point as well. Bad luck, I'd say. The short-faced bear, one way or another, was simply the victim of bad luck.

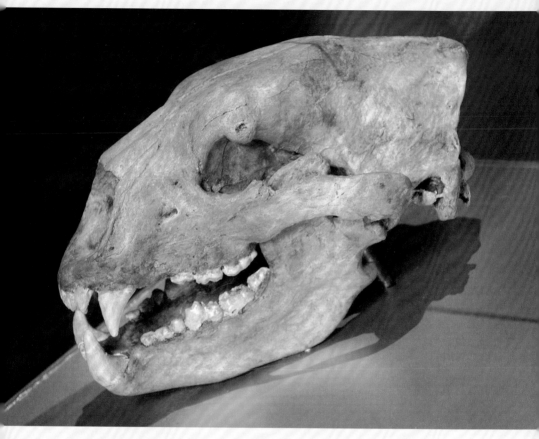

The skull of a short-faced bear. If you focus on the teeth, the face doesn't look short at all, but it was indeed relatively short compared to other bears.

Since the Ice Age

THE WORLD IS WARMING and climate change is a well-known topic these days, for the first time in history as far as I can tell. But to palaeontologists, climate change has been a hot topic, so to speak, for as long as the science has existed. Before there was talk of global warming, experts were reminding us that it wasn't long ago that our part of the world was locked in an ice age and was covered with sheets of glacial ice. Not only that, an Ice Age could always return and no one is certain whether these things happen gradually over hundreds or thousands of years, or suddenly and without much warning. It is common for people to assume that there is such a thing as a "normal" climate for Alberta and that this was the climate our ancestors discovered when the first aboriginal people came to Alberta after the Ice Age and the first Europeans arrived a few hundred years ago. Palaeontologists, however, paint a different picture. The great ice sheets of the Wisconsin Glaciation (the most recent period of major glaciation) melted away some 10,000 years ago. For a while, there were huge lakes and massive outflow channels draining glacial meltwater off the province. Then things settled down and the plants and animals began to re-colonize the landscape. But the climate was never really stable. For example, most studies show that Alberta was much warmer and drier about 4–6,000 years ago, when almost all of our lakes quite literally dried up. After a cooler period, another well-known climate shift occurred during the so-called "Little Climatic Optimum," from 900–1200 AD, when things were apparently warmer and the winters mild. Then, during the "Little Ice Age" from 1300–1850 the climate was much cooler. There are accounts of the Thames River freezing up in London, something that doesn't happen today. Also, various people who made attempts at agriculture during this time found that they could no longer grow crops. So no, there is no such thing as "normal" when it comes to climate, although I for one would prefer to let nature do the shifting, rather than carelessly leaving it to such things as greenhouse gasses.

A mountain glacier is like a mountain stream—it changes. Is the retreat of glaciers today an irreparable loss? Perhaps, or perhaps they will advance again someday.

Snakes of the Dinosaur Times

DURING THE LATE CRETACEOUS, many reptiles such as crocodilians, turtles and especially lizards were much like those we see today elsewhere in the world. Snakes, however, are a different story. Today, there are almost as many species of snakes on Earth as there are lizards (about three thousand snakes and perhaps four and a half thousand lizards). In other words, snakes have been a very successful group of animals. In fact, the ancestors of the first snakes were lizards and some biologists see snakes as nothing more, or less, than highly modified lizards themselves. This is the perspective I got from talking with Dr. Michael Caldwell of the University of Alberta. Dr. Caldwell has studied fossil snakes around the world, and I was surprised when he told me that from what we can see, the first snakes lived in water and still had hind legs. And during the Age of Reptiles there were not very many snakes at all. From what we can see in the fossil record, the evolution of snakehood did not immediately lead to the success and diversification of snakes. Among the fossils of Late Cretaceous animals from Alberta, there is only one sort of snake and it is known only from a few vertebrae (backbones). This is enough, however, to identify the fossils as snakes, and they have been given the name *Coniophis*. From the shape of *Coniophis* vertebrae, it is assumed by many palaeontologists that they were burrowing snakes, related to a sort of false coral snake that lives in South America today, *Anilius scytale*. Oddly, the fossils of *Coniophis* are absent from our best dinosaur-age fossil beds, the badlands of Dinosaur Provincial Park. *Coniophis* snakes were present both before and after the time when the Dinosaur Park rocks were laid down, and they survived well into the Age of Mammals. But their absence about 75 million years ago is a puzzle. For those who think that Alberta is not a very good place for reptiles today, it is amazing indeed to know that there are more types of snakes in Dinosaur Provincial Park today than there were during the time of the dinosaurs—bull snakes, prairie rattlesnakes, wandering garter snakes and plains garter snakes, to be specific. For a naturalist like me, that's just plain great news.

A bullsnake—one of the biggest snakes in North America, and a common species in southern Alberta. There may be more snakes here now than there were in dinosaur times.

Soft-shelled Turtles

SOFT-SHELLED TURTLES are common fossils in the badlands of southern Alberta. Those of us who have spent time searching for fossils in Alberta's Late Cretaceous rocks, from near the end of the Age of Dinosaurs, know that many of the animals that lived here alongside the dinosaurs have living relatives in the swamps and bayous of the American Southeast. That includes soft-shelled turtles. As the Bearpaw Sea retreated from eastern Alberta at the end of the Age of Dinosaurs, it shrank down to its present state and became the Gulf of Mexico, and along with it went alligators, sturgeon, garfish, and yes, soft-shelled turtles. This family of turtles is found around the world in warm climates now, and in North America they are most common in the Mississippi drainage, all the way to southern Ontario. Soft-shelled turtles are wonderful creatures with a bony shell that is partly or entirely covered by skin. Their heads are also distinctive, with nostrils that are situated at the tip of a pointy snorkel-snout that allows the turtle to hide under water and breathe only through this easily concealed tube. Was this an adaptation to avoid getting eaten by *Albertosaurus*? Probably not, but it's fun to look at a living soft-shelled turtle and think of how these animals survived during the dinosaur times. One thing I can assure you, they can bite very hard! But survival is about more than that. For me, the living fossil status of this animal really sank in the first time I saw a living Florida Soft-shelled Turtle in Florida. I was by that time deeply familiar with the texture and shape of fossil pieces of soft-shelled turtle shells from Alberta, and there in front of me was a living turtle with what looked exactly like fossils right there in the exposed portions of its shell. Whatever these turtles are doing they are doing it right, and to palaeontologists it is amazing that they have changed so little over such incredibly long periods of time.

A soft-shelled turtle, photographed on a lawn in south Texas while she was looking for a place to lay her eggs—an annual event for more than 100 million years.

Stegoceras

STEGOCERAS—not "Steg-o-SAUR-us" but "steg-OSS-err-ass!" *Stegoceras* was a dome-headed dinosaur, meaning that its skull was incredibly thick. This was a small dinosaur, about the size of a small person, but with a skull at least five centimetres thick. *Stegoceras* was the first of the so-called "dome-headed dinosaurs" to be discovered, way back in 1902, and it was a member of a family of similar creatures that lived throughout the Northern Hemisphere during the Cretaceous Period. In 1921, George Sternberg at the University of Alberta discovered the first nearly complete skeleton of a *Stegoceras* in what is now Dinosaur Provincial Park. When Charles Gilmore announced the discovery to science in 1924, other palaeontologists doubted that such a massive skull could have gone with such a slim, wimpy-looking body. For 50 years Alberta's *Stegoceras* skeleton remained the only specimen of its kind, until another dome-headed dinosaur skeleton was discovered in the Gobi Desert of Mongolia and our scientists were vindicated. Today, you can see the original fossils of *Stegoceras* in the University of Alberta's Palaeontology Museum and the reconstructed skeletons of these animals in lifelike poses at the Royal Tyrrell Museum in Drumheller. Casts of the original *Stegoceras* skeleton have also been exhibited in other museums around the world. And why did these dinosaurs have such thick skulls? The usual explanation is that they used them to butt heads, like bighorn sheep, and to display to one another as well. This interpretation has been challenged many times, and indeed the evidence for it is slim, but so far it's still the only explanation we have, and it is therefore still the best. In general, weird-looking structures on animal heads turn out to be weapons for fighting with other members of the same species, or for simply intimidating other members of the same species, but clearly, dome-headed dinosaurs still guard some interesting secrets.

A Stegoceras *skeleton in full gallop, breathing hard with its mouth open and deftly balancing its overweight head.*

The Sternberg Family

THE MEN OF THE STERNBERG FAMILY were the most famous dinosaur hunters in the history of Canadian palaeontology. Americans by birth,
they were hired by the Geological Survey of Canada in 1912 to compete with
Barnum Brown of the American Museum of Natural History in New York.
Charles H. Sternberg was the father, and he taught the techniques of palaeontology to his three sons, George, Levi, and Charles M. (better known as
"Charlie"). George was actually working for the New York crew when the
great Alberta dinosaur rush began in 1910 and the heyday of the Sternbergs'
work in the Alberta badlands extended all the way to 1916. Charles senior
was a writer and published two books (*Life of a Fossil Hunter* and *Hunting
Dinosaurs in the Badlands of the Red Deer River, Alberta, Canada*). They
were very personal and, in places, quite religious. In some chapters,
Charles prayed to God to take him back to the Cretaceous Period, where
his daughter Maude, who had died tragically as a child, would join him to
explore the ancient world. The elder Sternberg had hoped that his books
would bring him fame and a career as a public speaker, but this only partly
came to pass. Still, the Sternberg legacy was secure. Young Charlie went
on to work for the National Museum of Natural History (now the Canadian
Museum of Nature) and was instrumental in setting up Dinosaur Provincial
Park here in Alberta, as well in as exploring the Peace River country for
dinosaurs. He died in 1981. Levi worked at the Royal Ontario Museum and
died in 1976. George worked at the University of Alberta and died in 1969.
By the time the Royal Tyrrell Museum opened in 1985, all of the Sternbergs
had passed away. Heroes in both Canada and their native US, they set the
stage for dinosaur palaeontology as we know it today.

Top: *Charles H. Sternberg, the father, poses proudly beside the frill of* Chasmosaurus. *Bottom left:
George Sternberg and the lower jaw of* Albertosaurus. *Bottom right: A portrait of "Charlie," Charles
M. Sternberg. See page 115 for a photo of the third son, Levi Sternberg.*

Sedimentology, the Science of Sediments

WHEN MOST PEOPLE THINK OF PALAEONTOLOGY and the study of
fossils, they quite naturally imagine scientists in search of new bones,
teeth and prehistoric beasts. Certainly, this is still an important aspect of
palaeontology, but now that we have been at it for a few hundred years, the
beasts are becoming better and better known. As a science, palaeontology
isn't just a matter of naming and classifying dinosaurs and other extinct
creatures. It is also an attempt to reconstruct the great story of life on
Earth. Hence, we need a way to tie all of the various fossil discoveries
together and for many people this means sedimentology. Sedimentologists
are concerned not just with the fossils, but also with the rocks in which
they lie. Fossils almost always occur in sedimentary rocks, formed when
water or wind lays down layers of mud, silt, sand or gravel. And since these
sediments behave in very predictable ways, according to the so-called Laws
of Physics, it is amazing what sedimentologists can tell us about the rocks
in which we find our fossils. They can tell us how old the rocks are and
whether the rocks came from a lake, pond, river, stream, ocean, beach,
sand dune or landslide. They can tell us how fast the current was moving,
or the wind, and in which direction. They can tell us whether the area was
wet, dry, seasonal, or uniform. In other words, they can tell us about the
context of fossils, and context is often the most important aspect of all. At a
recent symposium on the palaeontology of Dinosaur Provincial Park, a very
fine group of scientists reviewed what we have learned in over a century of
study. To me, one theme stood out above all the others: It was only when
the sedimentology of the park was studied in detail by Dr. Dave Eberth of
the Royal Tyrrell Museum and his colleagues that we were finally able to
put the fossil riches of Dinosaur Park into perspective. And if there is one
thing that palaeontology is good for, it's for giving us perspective.

Layers in the rock, like those at Dinosaur Provincial Park, tell a story as interesting as that of the
fossils—the story of sedimentology.

Sturgeon, A Living Fossil Fish

A SURGEON IS A TYPE OF PHYSICIAN—a sturgeon is a type of primitive fish. Here in Alberta, most anglers know that the big prairie rivers are home to the occasional Lake Sturgeon, and that a really large sturgeon can weigh as much as 48 kilograms, and measure a metre-and-a-half in length. (And yes, here in Alberta "Lake Sturgeon" are indeed only found in rivers.) They are slow-growing fish that can live to 100 years of age, and they are becoming less common as the years go by. Some people fish for them, but sturgeon fishing is carefully regulated so that we don't lose this interesting creature forever. But in the rocks of the Alberta badlands, above the flow of the lazy prairie rivers, the remains of fossil sturgeon have been waiting patiently for us to study them since the days of the dinosaurs. They are easy to recognize because sturgeon are armoured with several rows of large bony scales and have an asymmetrical tail like that of a shark, with a fleshy lobe extending into its upper regions. The oldest fossil sturgeon, in fact, are about as old as the oldest dinosaurs, dating back at least 200 million years, so it's not surprising to find them in our own 65–80 million year-old badland rocks. The fossil sturgeon bones we have uncovered alongside the remains of Alberta's Cretaceous dinosaurs are so similar to living sturgeon that they have been given the same genus name in Latin—*Acipenser*. Not all palaeontologists agree, however, and some feel that the same name can't be used for something 75 million years old and for its living relatives today. No matter how similar they look, they *must* deserve a different name after all that time!—which is, of course, rather contrary to how scientific nomenclature is supposed to operate! Since most of the skeleton of a sturgeon is made of cartilage, not bone, this sort of thing is very difficult to resolve with any certainty. But the fact remains that sturgeon are indeed what we like to call "living fossils" and a wonderful connection to our palaeontological past.

A young sturgeon explores its aquarium at the Royal Tyrrell Museum. Inset: Sturgeon researcher Roger Korth releases a huge (but not record-setting) lake sturgeon beneath cliffs that bear the remains of its dinosaur-aged relatives.

Styracosaurus, A Classic Alberta Dinosaur

STYRACOSAURUS is one of the classic Albertan dinosaurs—the rhino-like creature with the spiked frill on its neck and a long horn coming off the top of its nose. Every kid knows *Styracosaurus*, and for good reason—it's a very cool dinosaur! *Styracosaurus* was described by the great Canadian palaeontologist Lawrence Lambe in 1913, and so far this creature is known only from the rocks of Dinosaur Provincial Park in southern Alberta. Its full name is *Styracosaurus albertensis*, and *albertensis* means "from Alberta." The meaning of *Styracosaurus* itself is a bit trickier—*saurus* means lizard, and *styrax* refers to the spike at the base of a spear shaft in the weaponry of ancient Greece. Not just any spike—those particular spikes. *Styracosaurus* were closely related to two other famous horned dinosaurs from Alberta, *Centrosaurus* and *Pachyrhinosaurus*, and all were about six metres long. So far, we only know of two complete *Styracosaurus* skulls, despite the fact that the head of *Styracosaurus* is one of the most recognizable dinosaur faces on Earth. In comic books and science fiction stories, *Styracosaurus* are often depicted with people riding on their backs, holding onto the frill horns and steering the dinosaur as if it had handlebars. I kind of like the idea, myself. In Dinosaur Provincial Park, there is a *Styracosaurus* bonebed: a deposit made up almost exclusively of the jumbled bones and teeth of *Styracosaurus*. This bonebed is not as well known as the more famous *Centrosaurus* bonebed in the same park or the *Pachyrhinosaurus* bonebed from Grande Prairie, but it seems to tell a similar story. It is intriguing that these three closely related sorts of dinosaurs have all produced bonebed deposits. Dr. Dave Eberth of the Royal Tyrrell Museum and his colleagues have suggested, based on their analysis of the bonebeds, that huge tropical storms and floods were the events that led to the formation of the horned dinosaur bonebeds. These storm surges would have been something like those that occasionally devastate the country of Bangladesh or the recent flooding of New Orleans. But in order to produce bonebeds dominated by one species of dinosaur, that species had to be very common and densely populated in the area at the time the bonebed was formed. So yes, we are justified in imagining huge so-called "herds" of *Styracosaurus*, *Centrosaurus* and *Pachyrhinosaurus*.

A model of *Styracosaurus* that once stood at Dinosaur Provincial Park—many people's favourite photo spot when they visit the Field Station of the Royal Tyrrell Museum.

Trace Fossils

THE STUDY OF FOSSILS is not merely the study of bodies and body parts turned to stone. It can also involve the study of what we call "trace fossils," the traces left behind when the animals were alive. The most famous of these are probably dinosaur tracks and Alberta has produced quite a few isolated dinosaur footprints, as well as a few trackways, from which we can deduce things about how dinosaurs walked and what they did when strolling across mudflats and the like. The great thing about tracks, as opposed to bones and teeth, is that tracks generally tell you about the living animal that made them, as opposed to the dead animal that constitutes a typical fossil. Of course, dinosaurs were not by any means the only animals that left tracks and traces. Other animals also had feet, and left footprints, and handprints too for that matter. Or nose-marks, butt drags, and belly furrows. Some ancient creatures lived in burrows, and there is an entire science of burrow analysis, based largely on such things as worms, insects, and crustaceans. Since it is often difficult to match up a trace fossil with the creature that made it, trace fossils are given a separate set of names. I asked Dr. Murray Gingras of the University of Alberta, what he thought the most impressive trace fossils in Alberta might be. Without hesitation, he told me about *Ophiomorpha*—petrified shrimp burrows lined with sand (and poop-balls made by shrimp) some 74 million years ago and preserved in rocks near Drumheller. "It was the New York City of shrimp, John," he told me, and as he spoke I pictured the vast tidal mudflats of the Bearpaw Sea, stretching up and down what is now central Alberta, dotted with millions of mud heaps, each home to a happy shrimp, and each shrimp certain that this was the way it would be for all time to come.

Dinosaur footprints in the rock near Grande Cache. These are obvious trace fossils, but many more subtle examples are still of great interest to palaeontologists.

Troodon, The "Smart" Dinosaur

TROODON IS A FAMOUS DINOSAUR with a long and intriguing history.
It was originally named by Joseph Leidy on the basis of a single tooth,
way back in 1856. Then, in the 1920s, palaeontologists announced that
Troodon was in fact a plant-eating, dome-headed dinosaur and that a skull
from Alberta possessed the same sort of teeth. It turned out that this was
a mistake. *Troodon* was actually a small meat-eater and the dome-head
(which we know as *Stegoceras*) had teeth that were similar, but not identical.
And to make things more confusing, plenty of real *Troodon* fossils were
being unearthed in Alberta and being called *Stenonychosaurus*, at least until
the 1980s. Now, we know *Troodon* as a reasonably common fossil from Late
Cretaceous rocks in western North America. It was a meat-eater, and it was
about two metres long. It stood on two legs and had a slender body, large
eyes, and grasping hands. In Asia, *Troodon* had many relatives. Beginning
in the 1970s, Dr. Phil Currie of the Royal Tyrrell Museum noticed that
Troodon and its relatives are also quite bird-like and used these similari-
ties to support the argument that birds were descended from dinosaurs. On
the other hand, Dr. Dale Russell, then at the Canadian Museum of Nature,
thought that perhaps *Troodon* was on the way to becoming humanoid, with
a large brain, upright stance and grasping hands. Extinction prevented this
from happening, Russell argued. Others pointed out that the large brain
was primarily devoted to processing information from the large eyes, that
Troodon walked like a bird, not like a human, and that plenty of animals
have grasping hands, but are otherwise not human-like. The fact remains
that *Troodon* was a success in its own right during the heyday of the Late
Cretaceous and was not the ancestor of anything else, as far as we can tell.
It lived more than 100 million years after the first birds evolved and it went
extinct at the end of the Age of Reptiles. Was it similar to the ancestor of
birds? Perhaps. Was it on the way to becoming human-like? As much as I
like and respect Dale Russell, I personally doubt it. And I can't help but add
that the very finest fossil I myself ever found was a partial skull of *Troodon,*
and it was this skull that inspired both Currie and Russell to begin the
process of making *Troodon* one of our best known dinosaurs. My role in the
story was minor, but I've watched it with interest all along.

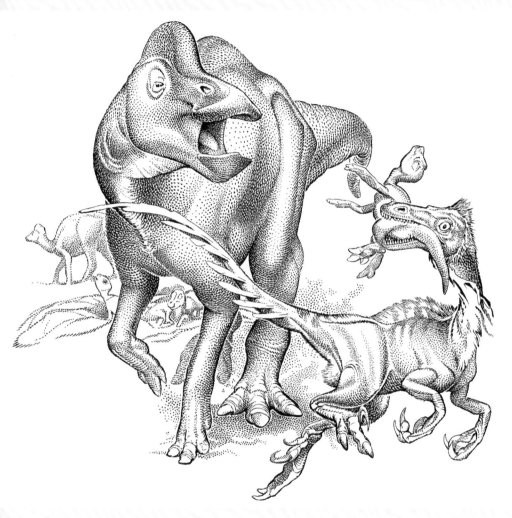

A speedy predator, Troodon *snatches a baby* Hypacrosaurus *from its nest, as the mother duck-bill bellows in protest.*

Triceratops at the Royal Tyrrell Museum. To get a sense of how magnificent it is, make sure to get down low and view it from the perspective of a small child!

Triceratops, The Three-horned Face

TRICERATOPS—what kid doesn't know this famous dinosaur, with its rhino-like body, heavy tail, three-horned head and bony frill to protect the neck? This is a VERY famous dinosaur! *Triceratops* was first named by the American palaeontologist Othniel Charles Marsh in 1889, but it is only within the last ten years that nearly complete skeletons of this dinosaur have been discovered. Before that, we were looking at composite skeletons pieced together from isolated bones. *Triceratops* fossils have been found in Wyoming, Montana, Colorado, South Dakota, Saskatchewan, and yes, in Alberta as well. In fact, the Royal Tyrrell Museum has recently excavated a lovely skull of *Triceratops* from Dry Island Buffalo Jump Provincial Park north of Drumheller. This may be the oldest *Triceratops* known, but *Triceratops* was one of the very last dinosaurs to live on Earth, just before the great extinction event 65 million years ago. It lived alongside *Tyrannosaurus rex* and the classic battle between *Triceratops* and *Tyrannosaurus* is a palaeontological cliché seen in dozens of paintings and movies. Usually, the hungry *Tyrannosaurus* foolishly attacks *Triceratops,* only to get poked in the belly by the *Triceratops'* horns, after which *Tyrannosaurus* goes away to lick its wounds and sulk. *Triceratops* the plant eater was probably quite an even match for *Tyrannosaurus* the meat eater, and they both weighed about five tonnes—about the same as a large African elephant. But palaeontologists now suspect that *Triceratops* and other horned dinosaurs used their horns and frill for displaying toward each other and scrapping with each other, as well as for protecting themselves from predators. Keep these things in mind when you re-enact this classic battle using plastic dinosaurs, since we all know how important it is, even to kids, to be fully, scientifically, accurate!

Tyrannosaurus or "T. rex"

TYRANNOSAURUS—THE WORLD'S MOST FAMOUS DINOSAUR. What can I tell you about this animal that you don't already know? Well, first, let's get clear on the distinction between *Tyrannosaurus*, *Tyrannosaurus rex*, and *T. rex*. Actually, they all refer to the same thing, unless you hold the opinion that there are two species of *Tyrannosaurus*—*Tyrannosaurus rex* in North America and *Tyrannosaurus bataar* in Asia. Most palaeontologists now call the Asian species *Tarbosaurus bataar*, which, of course, could also be abbreviated as *"T. bataar."* Those of us who are trained in such things avoid the use of abbreviations for genus names, unless it is clear which genus we are discussing, and the truth is that the phrase *"T. rex"* has done more to confuse the public about scientific names than just about any other example I can think of. To make matters even more complicated, as well as more interesting, my good friend, Dr. Brett Ratcliff, a scarab beetle specialist from Nebraska, decided to name a fossil scarab beetle *"Tyrannasorus rex"* as well. It's from the Dominican Republic, preserved in amber, and about 20 million years old. How can he do that, you ask, when each animal species has its own unique scientific name? Well, he did it by spelling the name "-a-sorus," not "-a-saurus." The dinosaur name means "tyrant lizard," while the beetle name means "tyrannical hump," referring to the mound of sap in which the beetle was killed. And yes, in the proper context they are both *"T. rex,"* which should convince you that these sorts of abbreviations can indeed lead to confusion. Names aside, *Tyrannosaurus rex* (the dinosaur) was one of the largest land predators ever to live at 14 metres or more in length and a weight of six tonnes or more. It lived in Alberta and throughout the American west, and went extinct at the end of the Age of Dinosaurs, 65 million years ago. Some think it may have been a scavenger, not a predator, and perhaps they are correct. But in many ways, I'd rather not raise that possibility here, since there's no easier way to get into an argument with every six-year-old kid in Alberta who reads this book.

No matter what pose it is mounted in, the skeleton of Tyrannosaurus rex is immediately recognizable to dinosaur enthusiasts around the world.

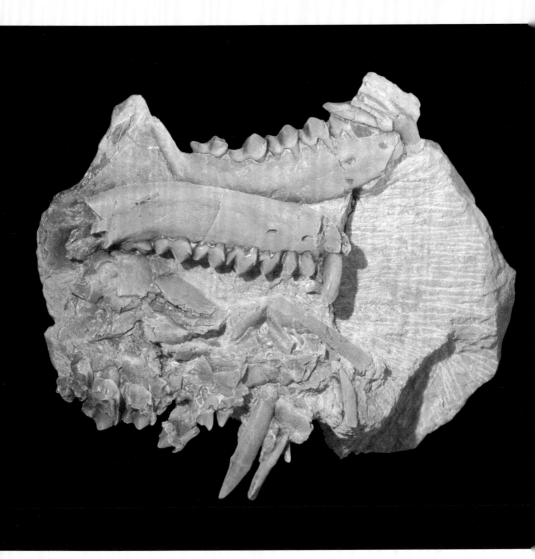

The somewhat crushed but beautifully preserved jaws of Bisonalveus browni, the venomous mammal from 60 million years ago that was found near Cochrane.

The Venomous Mammal

Perhaps you heard the news in 2005 of the discovery here in Alberta of a venomous small mammal dating from just after the Age of Reptiles, some 60 million years ago. Two of the best sites in Alberta for fossilized mammal teeth from this period are situated near Cochrane in the foothills and along the Blindman River near Red Deer. In the 1980s, Gordon Youzwyshyn, then a graduate student at the University of Alberta, studied the Cochrane fossils and set aside some peculiar specimens that appeared to be canine teeth with a channel in the enamel—clearly intended to carry venom, like a venomous snake fang. Gord knew they were something special, but the specimens were not complete enough for a full scientific study. More recently, a University of Alberta team unearthed a partial skull from the Blindman River shales, which also possessed grooved teeth for venom delivery, but with a different shape than the Cochrane teeth. These were identified as *Bisonalveus browni*, a mammal that was originally described by C. L. Gazin of the Smithsonian Institution in 1956 on the basis of its much less interesting molar teeth. Then in 2005, a paper on the new skull, written by Richard Fox of the University of Alberta and his graduate student, Craig Scott, appeared in the journal *Nature*. Their paper created a great deal of media interest because, as Fox and Scott pointed out, some living shrews have venomous saliva, although none have the snake-like fangs seen in these fossils. So what does this tell us about the evolution of mammals? Usually, when we think of venomous fangs, we think of the cute fuzzy mammal on the receiving end of a snake bite, but during the Palaeocene Era, some mammals had fangs too. And yet this wonderful adaptation did not persist. Just as with human affairs, perhaps having the deadliest weapons and the scariest face isn't any guarantee that one will triumph in the grand and complicated struggle for existence.

Glossary

Age of Dinosaurs: the Mesozoic Era, from 251 to 65 million years ago.

Age of Mammals: the Cenozoic Era, from 65 million years ago to the present day.

Age of Reptiles: the Mesozoic Era, from 251 to 65 million years ago.

Amphibian: a group of vertebrate animals with legs that develop from moist eggs that lack a waterproof shell.

Archosaur: a subgroup of the reptiles, characterized by a number of common features in their bone structure and including the crocodilians, dinosaurs, birds and a number of lesser-known extinct relatives.

Badlands: a landscape typified by bare hills, flat-topped hoodoos and rapidly eroding soft bedrock.

Bering, or Beringia: referring to the area that is now the Bering Strait between Alaska and Siberia, but was at many points in prehistory a land connection between the two continents.

Canine teeth: the teeth behind the incisors and before the premolars in a mammal skull. Canines are typically longer and more pointed than the other teeth and there are usually a total of four.

Cenozoic Era: the "Age of Mammals," from 65 million years ago to the present day.

Conodont: a group of primitive aquatic vertebrates, most closely related to lampreys, hagfish and other fishes. They were small, marine and had large teeth. They lived before the dinosaurs, from about 500 to 250 million years ago.

Dinosaur: a subgroup of the archosaurs, difficult to characterize except by technical details of bone structure, but including a variety of small to large terrestrial animals (including birds), but with no marine members and not including such things as thecodonts, pterosaurs, crocodilians, lizards, snakes, turtles, or tuataras.

DNA: the chemical that encodes the information that regulates the growth and development of animals and plants, technically known as deoxyribose nucleic acid (the old spelling), or deoxyribonucleic acid (the new).

Epoch: a time-based division of a geological period. The Palaeocene, Eocene, Oligocene, Miocene, Pliocene, and Pleistocene are all epochs within the Cenozoic Era.

Era: a major division of geological time, e.g., the Mesozoic Era, extending from 251 to 65 million years ago.

Erode, erosion: the action of water, wind, or ice wearing away at rocks and land.

Family: a group of related species, usually including many genera. All animal family names end in –idae, all plant family names end in –aceae.

Formation: a layer or "stratum" of rocks that may be quite thick and quite widespread and that is in a general way distinct from the layers above, beneath, and beside it.

Fossil: the remains of a once-living thing, preserved in sedimentary rocks.

Fossil record: the sum of what we know about fossil organisms, particularly their structure and anatomy, and their ages.

Genus (plural Genera): a group of closely related species.

Geological time: the great long span of time that encompasses the history of the planet Earth. Divisions of geological time are based on dates.

Geology: the study of the non-living Earth, at and below the surface.

Glacier: a thick sheet of ice, generally heavy enough to flow downhill at a very slow rate.

Ice Age: the Pleistocene Epoch, from 1.8 million years ago to 10,000 years ago.

Ichthyosaurs: an extinct group of marine reptiles that looked a great deal like dolphins, but with a tail fin that moved side to side, not up and down.

Invertebrate: an animal without a backbone.

Mammal: a vertebrate animal (including humans) possessing a suite of characteristic features, including hair, complex teeth and, in adult females, mammary glands for the production of milk to feed the young.

Mitochondrial: referring to the mitochondria—tiny rod-shaped components of animal and plant cells that produce the energy needed for body chemistry. Mitochondria evolved from parasitic bacterial cells, and for this reason they retain a separate strand of DNA not connected to the DNA of their host cell.

Organism: a living thing.

Palaeontology: the study of fossils.

Period: a time-based division of an era. For example, the Mesozoic Era is divided into the Triassic, Jurassic, and Cretaceous Periods.

Primate: a member of the mammal Order Primates, characterized by features of the teeth. Living examples include people, apes, monkeys, lemurs, and tarsiers, but there were many prehistoric squirrel-like primates as well.

Prokaryotic: the cells of bacteria and blue-green algae that lack such things as nuclei and mitochondria.

Reptile: a vertebrate animal with legs that develops from an egg with a waterproof shell that can survive on land (although in some the egg hatches internally and lacks a shell). Includes turtles, crocodilians, lizards, snakes, tuataras, archosaurs, and a variety of extinct groups as well.

Sandstone: rock formed from sand, held together by chemical cement.

Sedimentology: the study of sediments, such as silt, sand, and gravel and the rocks they turn into after they have been laid down by water or wind. The emphasis in sedimentology is on how the rocks were formed and in what sorts of environments.

Shale: rock formed from clay, silt, or mud held together by chemical cement.

Species: a group of living things that interbreed in the wild, or in palaeontology, a group of fossil plants or animals that look as if they would have interbred while alive.

Stratigraphy: the study of layers of rock, emphasizing attempts to date and correlate such layers. Like the closely related field of sedimentology, it is a branch of geology.

Vertebrate: an animal with a backbone.

Volcanic rocks: rocks produced by volcanoes, from such things as magma and ash.

References and Further Reading

MUCH OF THE INFORMATION that went into the preparation of this book came from personal contacts, web-based sources, and the collections and exhibits in the Royal Tyrrell Museum and other institutions. The references that follow are simply the most obvious items that are available in print and that were useful in preparing the text for the book.

Barnett, R., I. Barnes, M.J. Phillips, L.D. Martin, C.R. Harrington, J.A. Leonard, and A. Cooper. 2005. Evolution of the extinct sabretooths and the American cheetah-like cat. Current Biology. 15: R589-590.

Binns, Ronald. 1983. The Loch Ness Mystery Solved. Prometheus Books. New York. 228 pp.

Braman, D.R., F. Therrien, E.B. Koppelhus, and W. Taylor, eds. 2005. Dinosaur Park Symposium: short papers, abstracts, and programs. Special Publications of the Royal Tyrrell Museum, September 24-25, 2005, Drumheller, Alberta. 152 pp.

Brinkman, D.B., and E.L. Nicholls. 1993. New specimen of *Basilemys praeclara* Hay and its bearing on the relationships of the Nanhsiungchelyidae (Reptilia: Testudines). Journal of Paleontology. 67: 1027-1031.

Byers, J. A. 1998. American Pronghorn: Social Adaptations and the Ghosts of Predators Past. University of Chicago Press, Chicago. 318 pp.

Currie, P.J, and E.B. Koppelhus, eds. 2004. Dinosaur Provincial Park: A Spectacular Ancient Ecosystem Revealed. Indiana University Press, Bloomington, Indiana. 424 pp.

Currie, P.J, E.B. Koppelhus, M.A. Shugar, and J.L. Wright, eds. 2004. Feathered Dragons: Studies on the Transition From Dinosaurs to Birds. Indiana University Press, Bloomington, Indiana. 361 pp.

Fox, R.C. 1991. *Saxonella* (Primates, Plesiadapiformes) in North America: *S. naylori, sp. nov.* from the late Paleocene of Alberta, Canada. Journal of Vertebrate Paleontology. 11: 334-349.

Fox, R.C. and B.G. Naylor. 1982. A reconsideration of the relationships of the fossil amphibian *Albanerpeton*. Canadian Journal of Earth Sciences. 19: 118-128.

Fox, R.C., and C.S. Scott. 2005. First evidence of a venom delivery apparatus in extinct mammals. Nature. 435: 1091-1093.

Gardner, J.D., Russell, A.P. and D.B. Brinkman. 1995. Systematics and taxonomy of soft-shelled turtles (family Trionychidae) from the Judith River Group (Late Campanian) of North America. Canadian Journal of Earth Sciences. 32: 361-643.

Godfrey, J.D., ed. 1993. Edmonton Beneath our Feet: A Guide to the Geology of the Edmonton Region. Edmonton Geological Society. Edmonton. 150 pp.

Kieran, Monique. 2003. Reading the Rocks: A Biography of Ancient Alberta. Red Deer Press. Red Deer, Alberta. 128 pp.

Lillegraven, J.A., Z. Kielan-Jaworowska, and W. A. Clemens, eds. 1979. Mesozoic Mammals: the First Two-thirds of Mammal History. University of California Press, Berkeley. 311 pp.

Mussieux, R., and M. Nelson. 1998. A Traveler's Guide to Geological Wonders in Alberta. The Provincial Museum of Alberta, Federation of Alberta Naturalists and Canadian Society of Petroleum Geologists. Edmonton. 252 pp.

Poinar, G.O. Jr. 1993. Insects in amber. Annu. Rev. Entomol. 46: 145–159.

Ratcliffe, B.C., and F.C. Ocampo. 2001. *Tyrannosorus rex* Ratcliffe and Ocampo, a new genus and species of Miocene hybosorid in amber from the Dominican Republic (Coleoptera: Scarabaeoidea: Hybosoridae). Coleopterists Bulletin. 55: 351–355.

Spalding, D. 1999. Into the Dinosaur's Graveyard: Canadian Digs and Discoveries. Doubleday Canada, Toronto. 320 pp.

Sues, H.-D. 1978. A new small theropod dinosaur from the Judith River Formation (Campanian) of Alberta, Canada. Zoological Journal of the Linnaean Society. 62: 381–400.

Tanke, D.H. 2004. Mosquitoes and mud: the 2003 Royal Tyrrell Museum expedition to the Grande Prairie region (northwestern Alberta, Canada). Alberta Paleontological Society Bulletin. 19(2): 3–31.

Venczel, M., and J.D. Gardner. 2005. The geologically youngest albanerpetontid amphibian, from the lower Pliocene of Hungary. Paleontology. 48: 1273–1300.

Weishampel, D., P. Dodson, and H. Osmólska, eds. 2004. The Dinosauria, 2nd edition. University of California Press, Berkeley. 833 pp.

Wilson, M.V.H. 1980. Oldest known *Esox* (Pisces: Esocidae), part of a new Paleocene teleost fauna from Western Canada. Can. J. Earth Sci. 17: 307–312.

Key Figures in Alberta Palaeontology

Dr. Dennis R. Braman *(Curator of Palynology, Royal Tyrrell Museum)* studies fossil pollen and spores—microscopic clues that tell us about ancient plants, the changes that they underwent through time, variations in their occurrence because of changing climates and geographic location, and events surrounding the end-Cretaceous extinction event. He has integrated his studies with other researchers who study the earth's magnetic field, sedimentary rocks, chemistry, other fossil types, radiometric dating, and such exotic objects as "shocked quartz", micro-diamonds, and unusual amino acids (all three thought to originate with meteorite impacts).

Dr. Donald B. Brinkman *(Curator of Vertebrate Palaeontology and Head of Research Programs, Royal Tyrrell Museum)* studies ancient reptiles, and turtles in particular, that lived during the time of the dinosaurs. He is also interested in what we can learn from vertebrate "microfossils"—the small isolated bones and teeth of vertebrate animals. Dr. Brinkman's hardworking style is an inspiration to many in the palaeontology community.

Dr. Michael W. Caldwell *(Associate Professor, University of Alberta)* studies the fossils of ancient snakes, lizards and marine reptiles from Alberta and around the world. He is also interested in the development of limbs, and the loss of limbs in animals such as snakes. He began his professional career at the Canadian Museum of Nature, replacing Dale Russell, and was hired by the University of Alberta in 2000 upon the retirement of Richard Fox. A popular lecturer, Dr. Caldwell is having a profound effect on the next generation of palaeontologists.

Dr. Philip J. Currie *(Professor, University of Alberta and Research Associate, Royal Tyrrell Museum)* specializes in the systematics and paleobiology of theropod dinosaurs and is particularly interested in the origins of birds. He was instrumental in the origins of the Royal Tyrrell Museum, served for many years as the museum's Curator of Dinosaurs, and is almost a household name in Alberta. He has conducted fieldwork in Alberta, British Columbia, the Arctic, Antarctic, Argentina, Mongolia and China.

Dr. David A. Eberth *(Curator of Sedimentary Geology, Royal Tyrrell Museum)* studies the sedimentology and stratigraphy of the rocks that yield fossils, searching for clues about ancient climates, landscapes, and ecological systems, and how they have changed through time. Dr. Eberth's interpretations of dinosaur-bearing rocks in the badlands have reshaped our understanding of Earth history during the Cretaceous Period in Alberta.

Dr. Richard C. Fox *(Professor Emeritus, University of Alberta)* focuses his studies on mammals of the Cretaceous and Palaeocene Periods, but has also worked on a wide variety of vertebrate fossils other than mammals. Dr. Fox began work at the University of Alberta in 1965, and has been a central figure in Alberta palaeontology and has trained many of the people working at the Royal Tyrrell Museum.

Dr. James D. Gardner *(Collections Manager, Royal Tyrrell Museum)* manages the 120,000 plus specimens in the Museum's collection. This keeps him extremely busy, but he also finds time to pursue his scientific interests as well. His research focuses on the history and relationships of fossil frogs, salamanders and other amphibians.

Dr. Murray K. Gingras *(Associate Professor, University of Alberta)* is a specialist on trace fossils, and in particular the burrows of worms and other invertebrates. These can tell us a great deal about ancient environments and the forces that shaped the rock record of life on Earth, as well as the development of petroleum resources in Alberta's distant past. Dr. Gingras is an enthusiastic teacher as well as researcher, and is a continual inspiration to his students and colleagues.

Dr. Paul A. Johnston *(Mount Royal College and Research Associate, Royal Tyrrell Museum)* studies invertebrates, and has a particular interest in clams. Since invertebrates have always comprised the vast majority of animal life, an invertebrate palaeontologist's life is never dull. Dr. Johnston was for many years the Curator of Invertebrate Palaeontology at the Royal Tyrrell Museum.

Dr. Eva B. Koppelhus *(Research Associate, University of Alberta and Research Associate, Royal Tyrrell Museum)* studies ancient plant fossils as well as spores and pollen, and completed her training in Denmark, her home country. She also works closely with her husband, Philip Currie, and has thus become an important figure in the study of dinosaurs as well.

Dr. Bruce G. Naylor *(Director of the Royal Tyrrell Museum)* specializes in fossil amphibians and mammals. As Director of the Museum since 1991, Naylor has been instrumental in introducing many changes to the Museum's galleries. With a broad interest in natural history, Dr. Naylor sees the museum as more than just a showcase for fossils—it is also as a superb venue for telling the story of life on Earth.

Dr. Dale A. Russell *(Senior Curator of Palaeontology, North Carolina Museum of Natural Sciences)* Appointed to Ottawa's Canadian Museum of Nature in 1965 as Curator of Fossil Vertebrates, Russell then directed much of his attention to the dinosaurs of Dinosaur Provincial Park. The author of two very fine books on dinosaurs, Russell has had a creative and lasting impact on palaeontology around the world. Originally an American, Dr. Russell returned to the United States late in his career, and remains active in the study of dinosaurian ecology.

Dr. Ruth A. Stockey *(Professor, University of Alberta)* is interested in a wide variety of vascular plant fossils. She studies the anatomy and morphology of these plants in order to gain insights into plant evolution in general, and in particular the evolution of reproduction in coniferous trees and their relatives. As well, Dr. Stockey is interested in the interactions between plants and mycorrhizal fungi in the fossil record.

Dr. Mark V.H. Wilson *(Professor, University of Alberta)* is a vertebrate palaeontologist who teaches at the University of Alberta and studies ancient fish, including jawless fish of the Silurian and Devonian Periods and those that lived alongside the dinosaurs during the Cretaceous. He has also done fascinating work on fossil insects from the Palaeocene and Eocene Epochs. Much of his most influential work centres on ancient environments and taphonomy, the study of death and burial of ancient organisms.

Image Credits

page 3 Top: *Albanerpeton nexuosus, UALVP 16209, fused premaxillae, lingual view.* © Publications Scientifiques du Muséum National d'Histoire Naturelle, James Gardner; Middle: *Albanerpeton gracilis, RTMP 95.181.70 (holotype), incomplete left premaxill, labial and ligual view.* © Publications Scientifiques du Muséum National d'Histoire Naturelle. James Gardner; Bottom: *Albanerpeton gracilis, RTMP 96.78.103, anterior part of left dentary, lingual view.* © Publications Scientifiques du Muséum National d'Histoire Naturelle. James Gardner.

page 11 *Amia cf. A. pattersoni, UALVP 37150.* Mark Wilson, University of Alberta.

page 16 Steppe Bison. Species study by George "Rinaldino" Teichmann from Yukon Government Palaeontological Art Collection printed by permission of Rinaldino Art Studios, www.iceagebeasts.com.

page 19 Main: Blindman River near Blackfalds. John Acorn; Inset: *Saxonella naylori, UALVP 16201.* Craig Scott, University of Alberta.

page 23 Barnum Brown and Henry Fairfield Osborn. Image #17808. © American Museum of Natural History.

page 24 Burbank landscape. John Acorn.

page 27 Inset: Calgary skyline. Tourism Calgary.

page 28 *Camelops.* Species study by George "Rinaldino" Teichmann from Yukon Government Palaeontological Art Collection printed by permission of Rinaldino Art Studios, www.iceagebeasts.com.

page 31 Main: Canadian Shield near Sudbury, Ontario. John Acorn.

page 39 Extinct North American cheetah chasing a pronghorn. Michael Rothman.

page 40 Main: Bow Valley at Cochrane. John Acorn; Inset: *Chronoperates paradoxus, UALVP 32358.* Craig Scott, University of Alberta.

page 43 Brown Anole, St. Petersburg, Florida. John Acorn.

page 44 Main: American alligator, South Padre Island, Texas. John Acorn.

page 48 Devil's Coulee landscape. David Evans.

page 51 *Didelphodon coyi, TMP 84.64.1.* Craig Scott, University of Alberta.

page 52 Dinosaur Provincial Park near Brooks. Image #23_2902. © Travel Alberta.

page 56–57 Panorama showing nearly all of Drumheller, Alberta ca.1916 by G. Sternberg. Library and Archives Canada/Canada. Geographical Services Division collection/E002712853.

page 59 Top: Dry Island Buffalo Jump Provincial Park. John Acorn; Bottom: *Albertosaurus* bonebed quarry at Dry Island Buffalo Jump Provincial Park. John Acorn.

page 63 Cretaceous rocks in Edmonton. John Acorn.

page 64 *Edmontosaurus.* Donna Sloan, Royal Tyrrell Museum.

page 68 Model of *Caudipteryx* at the American Museum of Natural History. © American Museum of Natural History.

page 71 *Bombina orientalis,* the Oriental Fire-bellied "Toad." Captive individual. John Acorn.

page 80 Kleskun Hill Park, near Grande Prairie. Image #35_104D. © Travel Alberta.

page 83 Main: Lawrence M. Lambe. Image #GSC 109384. Reproduced with the permission of the Minister of Public Works and Government Services Canada, 2006 and Courtesy of Natural Resources Canada, Geological Survey of Canada.

page 92 Writing-on-Stone Provincial Park. Dennis Braman, Royal Tyrrell Museum.

page 96 Top: *Ptilodus reconstruction.* Valter Fogota; Bottom: *Ptilodus gnomus, UALVP 45145.* Craig Scott, University of Alberta.

page 100 Top: The Huxley, Alberta skeleton. Henry Fairfield Osborn. Image #17808. © American Museum of Natural History; Bottom: E.S. Christman's image of *Tyrannosaurus rex*. © American Museum of Natural History.

page 103 Oil sands near Fort McMurray, Alberta. Suncor Energy Inc.

page 115 Top: William A. Parks, Levi Sternberg and others. Image #A19640. © Provincial Archives of Alberta. Bottom: *Parksosaurus warranae*. © Natural History Museum, London.

page 116–117 *Esox tiemani, UALVP 15002 and PMS 69.38.50*. Mark Wilson, University of Alberta.

page 119 U-3 plant site/Dinosaur Quarry, Dinosaur Provincial Park. Dennis Braman, Royal Tyrrell Museum.

page 127 *Quetzalcoatlus*. Vladimir Krb, Royal Tyrrell Museum.

page 136 Columbia Icefield, Jasper National Park. Image #79_1648. © Travel Alberta.

page 141 Top & bottom: Spiny Soft-shelled Turtle near Mission, Texas. John Acorn.

page 144 Top: Charles H. Sternberg and a *Chasmosaurus belli* before being wrapped. ca. 1913 by G. Sternberg. Library and Archives Canada/National Museum of Canada collection/Accession 1979-298/Item 25421; Bottom left: Charles M. Sternberg. Image #GSC 80792. Reproduced with the permission of the Minister of Public Works and Government Services Canada, 2006 and Courtesy of Natural Resources Canada, Geological Survey of Canada; Bottom right: George Sternberg with lower jaw of a dinosaur, Steveville, Alberta, 1921. Glenbow Archives NA-3250-13.

page 147 Dinosaur Provincial Park, near Brooks. Image #04_9662. © Travel Alberta.

page 148 Inset: Lake Sturgeon and sturgeon researcher Roger Korth, in the South Saskatchewan River. Crystal Lively.

page 156 *Triceratops*. Chad Shier, Royal Tyrrell Museum.

page 160 *Bisonalveus browni* jaws. Craig Scott, University of Alberta.

Index

Also by John Acorn

Tiger Beetles of Alberta

0-88864-345-4

$19.95 paper

2001

Damselflies of Alberta

0-88864-419-1

$29.95 paper

2004

Ladybugs of Alberta

0-88864-381-0

$29.95 paper

2007

To learn more about the author, please visit www.acornthenaturenut.net.

"This excellent book by John Acorn delves into Alberta's past in a work that is a feast for the eyes and a challenge for the mind. The book covers everything one can imagine. [Along with dinosaurs,] there are insects trapped in amber, flying reptiles, fish, the wooly Mammoth, camels, and even a variety of lion. Most are accompanied by stunning photographs of the fossils themselves." —ALBERTA HISTORY

"Children and adolescents, plus their parents, will enjoy Deep Alberta. It is written with flair and an enthusiasm for the subject that is most engaging. The text is magnificently illustrated... One chapter has an excellent map showing the geology of Alberta. There are a number of teaching aids, including an index, a glossary, and an excellent list of references. An added feature, Key Figures in Alberta Palaeontology, gives brief biographies of the leading figures in the discipline. The organization of the book and the addition of the teaching aids make Deep Alberta suitable for classroom use....Highly Recommended." —CM MAGAZINE

"History book, science book, and bedtime storybook all in one! For its size, Deep Alberta is a book that would appeal to many readers on several levels. The range of topics covered in this concise format is broad, encompassing geography, biology, and geology as well.... Photos of dig sites give a good depiction of the kinds of terrain where fossils might be found, and in fact, one page is devoted to the topic 'How Do You Know Where to Dig.'"
—BOOK PLEASURES